Betty Crocker's
Slow Cooker
COOKBOOK

Macmillan • USA

MACMILLAN GENERAL REFERENCE USA
A Pearson Education Macmillan Company
1633 Broadway
New York, NY 10019-6785

Library of Congress Cataloging-in-Publication Data

Crocker, Betty.
  [Slow cooker cookbook]
  Betty Crocker's slow cooker cookbook.
    p.   cm.
  ISBN 0-02-863469-1
  1. Electric cookery, Slow.   I. Title   II. Title: Slow cooker cookbook.
  TX827.C75   1999   99-35736
  641.5'884—dc21   CIP

General Mills, Inc.

Betty Crocker Kitchens
Manager, Publishing: Lois L. Tlusty
Editor: Lois L. Tlusty
Recipe Development: Altanette Autry, Phyllis Kral
Food Stylists: Mary Johnson, Cindy Ojczyk, Carol Grones
Nutritionists: Nancy Holmes, R.D.
Photographic Services:
Art Director: Pam Kurtz
Photographer: Nanci Doonan Dixon

Cover and Book design by Michele Laseau

For consistent baking results, the Betty Crocker Kitchens recommend Gold Medal Flour

Manufactured in the United States of America
10 9 8 7 6 5 4 3
First Edition

Cover photo: Beef Stew with Sun-Dried Tomatoes (page 42)

Greetings—

Do you want dinner ready and waiting? Well, you've come to the right place. With your slow cooker and these easy flavor-packed recipes, you can get a jump start on dinner in the morning without much effort . Plus, you come home to the enticing aroma of a home-cooked meal. Best of all, you can relax—dinner just about makes itself!

Your slow cooker is not only for the work-a-day world but also for carefree entertaining. Slow cookers are ideal for serving a hot beverage, warm dip or on the buffet table because it keeps food hot and tasty for several hours. Look for this crowd-size symbol: next to recipes to serve the next time family and friends gather at your home.

Crowd SIZE

Your slow cooker is the perfect partner when you're on the go, too. Whether it's a scout's banquet, a party at work or a neighbor's potluck—you'll have no problem packing up your dish and keeping it hot.

So get ready to discover all the tasty simmered-in flavors of slow cooking.

Betty Crocker

P.S. I love my slow cooker!

C o n t e

n t s

Joy of Slow Cooking

Slow and Steady Cooking

In today's busy world, things just seem to be getting faster, including the time we spend preparing meals. What a surprise to discover that using a slow cooker is an answer to everyday dinner. Slow cooking is the best way to keep pace with our busy lives since the meal you're making requires little to no attention while it cooks, and you'll enjoy a home-cooked, good-for-you meal.

Designed for economy and ease as well as for comfort and convenience, this slow, steady cooking method fits into every life-style. Put the ingredients into the slow cooker, then cover and let it cook while you are at work, running errands, or enjoying the day outside. Small families and individuals can also enjoy the benefits of slow cooking, since you can make enough to enjoy "planned-overs" on another day. And nothing is quite as welcoming as coming home to the rich aroma of a home-cooked meal wafting through the house. Invest in the convenience and comfort of slow cooking. It offers a variety of advantages.

Energy Efficient

Slow cooking uses very little electricity because the wattage used is low. Consumers benefit because this is a low-cost way to prepare a meal.

Cool Cooking

Slow cooking isn't just for stews and soups during the winter. You can do it all year round, and without using the oven during the summer, the kitchen stays cooler. It's also great when your oven is in use and you want to make side dishes or desserts.

Perfectly Portable

A slow cooker is the perfect appliance for motor homes, to take to the cabin and for college students. It eliminates the need for multiple pots and pans. It is great to carry along to potlucks, parties and other social events because your dish will stay warm.

No Clock Watching

If you are stuck in traffic or running late for an appointment, not to worry! An extra half or full hour on the low setting will not ruin a meal in the slow cooker.

Easy Preparation

Cut vegetables and meat when you have the time (you can even brown the meat ahead of time!), wrap them separately and refrigerate, then place them in the slow cooker the next morning. Dinner will be ready and waiting when you get home, and even you will be surprised by how easy it was!

Moist and Flavorful

Slow cooking allows the juices of foods to blend and create tender, flavorful dishes, and the meat generally shrinks less.

Make and Take

Office party or meeting with the troops? Wrap the slow cooker in a towel or newspaper to insulate it, and place it in a box that will stay flat in your car. Serve the food within an hour, or plug in the cooker and set it on the low heat setting so it will stay warm for hours.

Meals in Minutes

Slow-cooker meals cook themselves. When you add bread, a salad or a vegetable, and a beverage, the meal is ready to set on the table in minutes.

Slow-Cooking Savvy

Although using a slow cooker is pretty simple, boning up on the basics is a good idea so you'll be familiar with what slow cookers offer. Here's a brief rundown of the two types of slow cookers available, both designed to ensure even cooking with an automatic control.

Continuous Slow Cooker

The food cooks continuously at a very low wattage. The heating coils are in the outer metal shell. The coils become hot and stay on constantly to heat the crockery liner. This type of cooker has two or three fixed settings: low (about 200°), high (about 300°) and in some newer models, auto, which shifts from high to low automatically. The ceramic liner may be fixed or removable. Removable liners offer easy cleanup.

Intermittent Crockery Cooker

This cooker has a heating element in the base on which the cooking container stands. The heat cycles on and off (like an oven) to maintain a constant temperature. The cookers have a dial with numbers or temperatures. Be sure to follow the use-and-care book that comes with the cooker to determine what settings to use. Often, the lowest setting/temperature is only for keeping foods warm, not for cooking.

Slow cookers range in size from a 1- to 6-quart capacity. The 1-quart size is perfect for making and keeping dips and spreads warm for a party. The larger sizes are ideal for cooking one-dish meals and other family favorites. We have included a range of appropriate size cookers at the top of each recipe.

High or Low?

Most slow cookers have low and high control settings. At the low heat setting, the food temperature remains just below the boiling point. Many recipes use the low heat setting because the longer cooking time often fits better into your daily schedule. You can start dinner before leaving your home in the morning, and it is ready when you return.

At the high heat setting, liquid gently bubbles and cooks approximately twice as fast as on low heat. It is always best to use the heat setting that a recipe recommends, but sometimes you prefer a shorter cook time. Use the guide that 1 hour on high is equal to 2 to 2 1/2 hours of cooking on low. So if you don't have 8 to 10 hours for dinner to cook on the low heat setting, use high instead, and it should be ready to eat in 4 to 5 hours.

After the food is cooked, it can be held at the low heat setting up to an hour or so without overcooking. Remember, it is best to check occasionally to see whether it needs to be stirred.

A Watched Crock Never Cooks...

A slow cooker that's opened doesn't cook, so don't peek! Keep the cover on unless a recipe tells you to remove it. Removing the cover allows heat to escape and adds 15 to 20 minutes to the cooking time each time you peek.

How Full?

For best results, a slow cooker should be between one-half and three-fourths full of food. This helps to ensure that the liquid will not cook away during the long hours of cooking. It also helps keep the food moist and tender.

Finishing Cook Time

You'll see that some recipes have a "Finishing Cook Time" included. This is necessary when a slow cooker recipe isn't completely "self-sufficient" and a few minutes of additional cooking is required. It can be making fluffy dumplings on a hearty beef stew, adding pasta to soup or to thicken the juices to make a richer tasting sauce. We've brought this to your attention to let you know that someone will have to be around for those additional 15 to 30 minutes of cooking.

Oops! The Power's Out

What should you do if the power goes off and you aren't at home while your slow cooker is in use? It is best not to eat the food even if it looks done. If the power has been turned off for a length of time, the food may have stood at too low a temperature to be safe.

However, if you are home, you can put the uncooked food in another pan and finish cooking it on the stove, if it is gas, or on an outdoor grill. Or store it in a cooler with ice if the power might be off for some time and you have no way to continue cooking.

If you are home while using your slow cooker and you know the food is completely cooked, it can safely stay in the cooker up to 2 hours with the power off. Don't lift the lid so that the temperature won't drop.

Storing and Serving Leftovers

Be sure to remove any remaining food from the slow cooker within 1 hour after it is finished cooking and store it in the refrigerator. We recommend not reheating leftovers in the slow cooker because it takes too long for the food to reach a safe internal temperature. It is best to reheat leftovers in the microwave or on top of the stove.

If you made a dish ahead and stored in the refrigerator but want to serve it in the slow cooker, that is fine. Just reheat the food on top of the stove or in the microwave. Then put it in a preheated slow cooker to keep hot and to serve.

Adapt Your Favorite Recipes

One benefit of using a slow cooker is that you can adapt mom's favorite recipe for beef stew or your most-requested vegetarian chili recipe. There's no need to hunt for a new recipe! Using the following guidelines to help, you can adapt many of your favorite recipes for making in a cooker.

First, begin by finding a similar recipe in this cookbook. It will serve as a guide for quantities, amount of liquid and cooking time. Next, unless you're making a soup, decrease the amount of liquid in your recipe to about half because liquids do not boil away. For soups, simply leave liquid level as recommended.

You can make recipes that use less-expensive cuts of meat because they become very tender in the moist-heat, low-temperature slow cooker. It is a good idea to trim as much visible fat as possible from meat before cooking so there is less fat to remove from the finished dish before serving it.

If poultry isn't browned in a skillet before adding to the cooker, it is best to remove the skin first. This not only helps reduce calories, but it also improves the appearance of the cooked pieces. Always cook and drain any type of ground meat, whether it is beef, pork or poultry, before placing it in the slow cooker. The temperatures reached in a cooker may not become hot enough quickly enough to kill any bacteria that ground meats may contain.

Dense root vegetables, such as carrots, potatoes and turnips, often take longer than meat to cook when cooked together in a slow cooker. So cut them into small, bite-size pieces and place them in the bottom of the cooker. That way, the juices from the meat drip down and help the vegetables cook.

We have found that the flavor of dried basil strengthens during long cooking. If adapting a recipe using dried basil, we suggest that you cut the amount called for in half or add fresh basil during the last 30 minutes of cooking time.

Dairy products, such as milk, sour cream and cheese, break down during long cooking times, and the sauce will be curdled. Instead of using fresh milk, try canned condensed soups, nonfat dry milk powder or canned evaporated milk for a smooth, creamy sauce. For best results, add cream, sour cream or cheese during the last 30 minutes of cooking time or just before serving to prevent them from breaking down.

Finally, be sure to allow sufficient cooking time. Most soups, stews and one-dish meals require 8 to 10 hours on the low heat setting.

Secrets of the Slow Cooker

Little "secrets," or tips and tricks, often make a recipe come out just right! From a picture-perfect appearance to the fork-tender meat and delicious vegetables, these success tips help ensure each slow-cooked meal comes with a healthy dose of praise.

First Things First!

Spray the inside of the slow cooker with cooking spray for easy cleanup.

Root vegetables, such as carrots and potatoes, take longer to cook, so cut these vegetables into small pieces or thinly slice them and place in the bottom of the slow cooker for best results.

Remove the skin from poultry, and trim excess fat from meats to reduce excess fat in the finished dish and reduce calories.

Always cook and drain ground meats before adding them to the slow cooker.

Brown meats or poultry in a skillet before adding to the slow cooker. It isn't necessary, but it can enhance the flavor and appearance of the finished dish.

Thaw frozen vegetables or rinse them with warm water to separate before placing them in the slow cooker. Adding frozen vegetables will lower the internal temperature, and the dish will take longer to cook.

Full of Flavor

Use dried leaf herbs instead of ground because they keep more flavor during the long cooking time. Another way to ensure sufficient flavor is to stir in fresh herbs during the last hour of cooking. Always taste before serving to see whether additional seasoning is needed.

Concentrate the flavor of juices in the slow cooker by removing the lid and cooking on the high heat setting during the last 20 to 30 minutes.

To create a more pronounced flavor in soups and stews, substitute broth for the water or add bouillon cubes with the water.

Ground red pepper (cayenne) and red pepper sauce tend to strengthen and become bitter during long slow cooking. Use small amounts and taste during the last hour of cooking and decide whether more seasoning is needed.

Safety Check

For food-safety reasons, keep this checklist in mind as you use your slow cooker.

> Thaw meat and poultry in the refrigerator or in a microwave oven following the manufacturer's directions. Do not thaw at room temperature.

- Cook and drain all ground meat before adding it to the slow cooker to help destroy any bacteria that the meat may contain.

- We recommend not cooking whole poultry, such as chicken, turkey and Rock Cornish hens, in a slow cooker. It takes too long for a safe cooking temperature to reach the bone.

- Always remove leftovers from the slow cooker and refrigerate or freeze them as soon as you are finished eating. Cooked food shouldn't stand at room temperature longer than 1 hour.

- Don't undercook foods. For food-safety reasons, slow cooker recipes containing raw poultry or beef should cook a minimum of three hours.

- The temperature in the middle of the food being cooked must reach 140° within 1 1/2 hours and remain at or above 140° for at least 30 minutes at the setting used. For this reason, do not use frozen ingredients, and do not assemble recipes and refrigerate ahead of time. (But it is okay to prep the ingredients and refrigerate separately ahead of time. Just don't combine them until you are ready to cook.) Refrigerated ingredients, such as meat and poultry, can be used right from the refrigerator.

- To save time in the morning, you can peel and cut up vegetables and brown meat the night before. Put the vegetables and meat in separate containers, cover and refrigerate. They are ready to pop into the cooker in the morning.

Cooking Meats in Your Slow Cooker

Meats prepared in a slow cooker do not brown like they do when cooked in a skillet or an oven. Browning meats before placing them in the slow cooker isn't necessary, but browning in a skillet or under the broiler does help eliminate excess fat and produce the flavor that some people prefer.

For meats to cook evenly, allow spaces between pieces so the heat can circulate and seasonings can be distributed.

Coating pot roasts and stew meat with flour will help to thicken the liquid as it cooks.

Before serving pot roast, meaty soups or stews, skim off excess fat with a slice of bread or skim off with a spoon.

Thickening the Juices

Because slow cookers are closed during the entire cooking period, liquids don't easily evaporate. Therefore, flavorful juices develop as the food cooks. You can use the juices without thickening, or if you prefer, thicken it to make gravy. It takes a little extra time, but it's worth the effort!

To make gravy to serve with a roast, first remove the roast from the slow cooker; cover and keep it warm. Remove the juices from the cooker and measure 1 cup for each cup of gravy. Pour the juices into a saucepan. Mix together 1 tablespoon cornstarch and 1 tablespoon cold water for each cup of liquid. Stir mixture into juices in saucepan. Cook over medium heat, stirring occasionally, until mixture boils. Boil and stir 1 to 2 minutes or until slightly thickened.

For stews or other main dishes, you will want to thicken the entire dish. Turn the cooker to high heat setting. For each 2 cups of liquid, mix 1/4 cup all-purpose flour and 1/4 cup cold water. Or if you prefer cornstarch, mix 2 tablespoons cornstarch and 2 tablespoons cold water for each 2 cups liquid. Stir mixture into the cooker. Cover and cook 20 to 30 minutes.

Beans, Beans!

Cooking dried beans in a slow cooker can be tricky because of the variations in electrical power and the types of minerals found in your local water. Beans need sufficient heat to tenderize them; dried beans cooked on the low heat setting for 8 to 10 hours may not be tender. We found three ways to cook dried beans, and you can select the one that best fits your schedule. The most convenient way to cook a dried bean recipe is to put all the ingredients into the slow cooker and cook on the high heat setting until the beans are tender. We used this method for most of the dried bean recipes.

Another method is to cook the beans 2 to 3 hours on the high heat setting, then reduce to the low heat setting for 8 to 10 hours. This is a little less convenient because you have to be available after a couple of hours to reduce the heat setting.

A more traditional method for cooking dried beans is to first place the beans and water in the slow cooker. Cover and cook on the high heat setting 2 hours. Turn off the cooker, and let beans stand 8 to 24 hours. Change the water. Add remaining ingredients, and cook on the low heat setting 8 to 12 hours or until done. We used this method for the Old-Fashioned Baked Beans recipe on page 140 because this allows the flavors to blend and offers more of an oven-baked taste.

High Altitude Tips

For people who live at higher altitudes (3,500 feet and above), everyday cooking has some challenges, and slow cooking is no exception. Unfortunately, trial and error often is the only way to make improvements because no set rules apply to all recipes.

Here are some guidelines to keep in mind when using your cooker:

Most foods will take longer to cook, particularly meats cooked in boiling liquid. Sometimes it takes twice as long than the recipe suggests for meats to become tender. You might want to try cooking meats on high heat setting rather than low to help shorten the cooking time.

Cutting vegetables into smaller pieces than suggested in the recipe will help them cook more quickly.

Dried beans also will cook more slowly. We recommend using the method of soaking them overnight in water before cooking in the slow cooker.

You can call your local U.S. Department of Agriculture (USDA) Extension Service office, listed in the phone book under county government, with questions about slow cooking at high altitude.

Simmering One-pot Meals

◄ *Burgundy Stew with Herb Dumplings (page 44)*

13

Vegetable Minestrone

■ 8 servings ■

SLOW COOKER:
3 1/2- to 6-quart

PREP TIME:
20 minutes

COOK TIME:
Low 7 to 9 hours
High 3 1/2 to 4 1/2 hours

FINISHING COOK TIME:
High 15 to 20 minutes

Ingredient Substitution

The kids will love the little corkscrew rotini pasta in this vegetable-packed soup, but elbow macaroni—that good old standby—works just as well.

Serving Suggestion

Minestrone means "big soup," and this big soup needs only thick slices of a seedy whole-grain bread to make a "big meal."

Finishing Touch

Adding the snap pea pods at the beginning with the other vegetables makes this soup easy, but if you like a brighter green, add them with the pasta at the end. Or if you don't have any pea pods, just leave them out, and your soup still will be colorful and tasty.

1 medium yellow summer squash, cut lengthwise in half, then cut crosswise into 1-inch pieces

2 medium carrots, cut into 1/4-inch slices (1 cup)

1 medium bell pepper, chopped (1 cup)

1 cup snap pea pods

1/3 cup chopped onion

4 cups water

1 jar (25 1/2 ounces) marinara sauce

1 can (15 to 16 ounces) kidney beans, rinsed and drained

1 1/2 cups uncooked rotini pasta (4 1/2 ounces)

1 teaspoon sugar

1 teaspoon salt

1/4 teaspoon pepper

Shredded Parmesan cheese, if desired

1. Mix squash, carrots, bell pepper, pea pods, onion, water, marinara sauce and beans in 3 1/2- to 6-quart slow cooker.

2. Cover and cook on low heat setting 7 to 9 hours (or high heat setting 3 1/2 to 4 1/2 hours) or until vegetables are tender.

3. Stir in pasta, sugar, salt and pepper.

4. Cover and cook on high heat setting 15 to 20 minutes or until pasta is tender. Sprinkle each serving with cheese.

1 Serving: Calories 260 (Calories from Fat 35); Fat 4g (Saturated 1g); Cholesterol 0mg; Sodium 920mg; Carbohydrate 53g (Dietary Fiber 7g); Protein 10g

% Daily Value: Vitamin A 32%; Vitamin C 30%; Calcium 6%; Iron 20%

Diet Exchanges: 3 Starch, 1 Vegetable

Creamy Leek and Potato Soup

■ 8 servings ■

SLOW COOKER:
3 1/2- to 6-quart

PREP TIME:
20 minutes

COOK TIME:
Low 8 to 10 hours
High 4 to 5 hours

FINISHING COOK TIME:
Low 20 to 30 minutes

6 medium leeks (2 pounds), thinly sliced

4 medium potatoes (1 1/2 pounds), cut into 1/2-inch cubes

2 cans (14 1/2 ounces each) ready-to-serve chicken or vegetable broth

1/4 cup margarine or butter

1/2 teaspoon salt

1/4 teaspoon pepper

1 cup half-and-half

Chopped fresh chives, if desired

1. Mix all ingredients except half-and-half and chives in 3 1/2- to 6-quart slow cooker.

2. Cover and cook on low heat setting 8 to 10 hours (or high heat setting 4 to 5 hours) or until vegetables are tender.

3. Pour vegetable mixture by batches into blender or food processor. Cover and blend on high speed until smooth; return to cooker. Stir in half-and-half.

4. Cover and cook on low heat setting 20 to 30 minutes or until hot. Sprinkle with chives.

1 Serving: Calories 190 (Calories from Fat 90); Fat 10g (Saturated 3g); Cholesterol 10mg; Sodium 720mg; Carbohydrate 22g (Dietary Fiber 3g); Protein 6g

% Daily Value: Vitamin A 12%; Vitamin C 16%; Calcium 8%; Iron 12%

Diet Exchanges: 1 Starch, 1 Vegetable, 2 Fat

Betty's Success Tip

Leeks grow best in sand soil and the broad, flat leaves of a leek wrap around each other, making the perfect place for sand to hide. The easiest way to remove the sand is to cut the leek lengthwise, almost to the root end. Hold the leek under cool running water while fanning the leaves, so the water can wash out the sand.

Ingredient Substitution

Leeks are very tasty but do take a few more minutes to clean. To save time, use a chopped large onion instead of the leeks. Or use a chopped medium onion and, for a little color, 1/2 cup sliced green onions.

Serving Suggestion

This is really an all-season soup. Serve it warm on a chilly evening, and sprinkle each serving with crumbled cooked bacon to added a hearty smoke flavor. Or in the summer, chill it in the refrigerator, and you'll have a delicious, refreshing chilled soup ready to enjoy on the deck.

French Onion Soup

■ 8 servings ■

SLOW COOKER:
3 1/2- to 6-quart

PREP TIME:
50 minutes

STARTING COOK TIME:
High 30 to 35 minutes

COOK TIME:
Low 7 to 9 hours
High 3 to 4 hours

3 large onions, sliced (3 cups)

3 tablespoons margarine or butter, melted

3 tablespoons all-purpose flour

1 tablespoon Worcestershire sauce

1 teaspoon sugar

1/4 teaspoon pepper

4 cans (14 1/2 ounces each) ready-to-serve beef broth

Cheesy Broiled French Bread (below)

1. Mix onions and margarine in 3 1/2- to 6-quart slow cooker.

2. Cover and cook on high heat setting 30 to 35 minutes or until onions begin to slightly brown around edges.

3. Mix flour, Worcestershire sauce, sugar and pepper. Stir flour mixture and broth into onions. Cover and cook on low heat setting 7 to 9 hours (or high heat setting 3 to 4 hours) or until onions are very tender.

4. Prepare Cheesy Broiled French Bread. Place 1 slice bread on top of each bowl of soup. Serve immediately.

Betty's Success Tip

Here's some "broth math" to help you if don't have any ready-to-serve beef broth on hand. You can use three 10 1/2-ounce cans of condensed beef broth with 2 1/2 soup cans of water or 7 cups of your homemade beef broth. Or add 7 cups of water with 7 beef bouillon cubes or 2 heaping table-spoons of beef bouillon granules.

Ingredient Substitution

Vegetarians in your family? Use 4 cans of ready-to-serve vegetable broth instead of the beef broth. The color will not be a rich, deep brown, though, so Golden French Onion Soup may be a more appropriate name!

Cheesy Broiled French Bread

8 slices French bread, 1 inch thick

3/4 cup shredded mozzarella cheese (3 ounces)

2 tablespoons grated or shredded Parmesan cheese

Set oven control to broil. Place bread slices on rack in broiler pan. Sprinkle with cheeses. Broil with tops 5 to 6 inches from heat about 3 minutes or until cheese is melted.

1 Serving: Calories 185 (Calories from Fat 70); Fat 8g (Saturated 3g); Cholesterol 5mg; Sodium 1240mg; Carbohydrate 21g (Dietary Fiber 2g); Protein 9g

% Daily Value: Vitamin A 6%; Vitamin C 2%; Calcium 14%; Iron 8%

Diet Exchanges: 1 Starch, 2 Vegetable, 1 Fat

Borscht

■ 6 servings ■

SLOW COOKER:
3 1/2- to 6-quart

PREP TIME:
10 minutes

COOK TIME:
Low 6 to 8 hours
High 3 to 4 hours

Betty's Success Tip

Shredding cabbage is easy when you use a long, sharp knife. Cut the cabbage into fourths, and remove the core. Thinly slice the fourths by cutting across the leaves to make long, thin strips.

Ingredient Substitution

Instead of shredding cabbage, you can use cabbage slaw mix found in the produce section of the supermarket. If other vegetables, such as shredded carrots, are in the mix, they will just add to the flavor of the soup.

Serving Suggestion

This streamlined version of the colorful eastern European favorite can be served hot or chilled. Serve it hot tonight for dinner. Any leftover soup will be ready in the refrigerator for a quick, no-fuss lunch.

2 cans (16 ounces each) diced beets, undrained

2 cans (10 1/2 ounces each) condensed beef broth

1 small onion, finely chopped (1/4 cup)

2 cups shredded cabbage

1 tablespoon sugar

1 tablespoon lemon juice

3/4 cup sour cream, if desired

Chopped fresh dill weed, if desired

1. Mix all ingredients except sour cream and dill weed in 3 1/2- to 6-quart slow cooker.

2. Cover and cook on low heat setting 6 to 8 hours (or high heat setting 3 to 4 hours) or until cabbage is tender.

3. Top each serving with sour cream and dill weed.

1 Serving: Calories 70 (Calories from Fat 10); Fat 1g (Saturated 0g); Cholesterol 0mg; Sodium 720mg; Carbohydrate 15g (Dietary Fiber 3g); Protein 3g

% Daily Value: Vitamin A 0%; Vitamin C 12%; Calcium 4%; Iron 16%

Diet Exchanges: 3 Vegetable

Chicken and Rice Gumbo Soup

■ 6 servings ■

SLOW COOKER:
3 1/2- to 6-quart

PREP TIME:
30 minutes

COOK TIME:
Low 7 to 8 hours

FINISHING COOK TIME:
Low 20 minutes

3/4 pound skinless, boneless chicken thighs, cut into 1-inch pieces

1/4 pound fully cooked smoked sausage (two 5-inch sausages), chopped

2 medium stalks celery (with leaves), sliced (1 1/4 cups)

1 large carrot, chopped (3/4 cup)

1 medium onion, chopped (1/2 cup)

1 can (14 1/2 ounces) stewed tomatoes, undrained

5 cups water

2 tablespoons chicken bouillon granules

1 teaspoon dried thyme leaves

1 package (10 ounces) frozen cut okra, thawed and drained

3 cups hot cooked rice, for serving

Hot red pepper sauce

Betty's Success Tip

Forget to put the okra in the refrigerator to thaw? No problem. To quickly thaw it, rinse under cold running water until it is separated and thawed.

Ingredient Substitution

We like the heartier flavor of the chicken thighs in this gumbo, but you can use the same amount of skinless, boneless chicken breast.

Finishing Touch

The red pepper sauce will lose its punch if it is added to the gumbo at the beginning of cooking. Pass the bottle of pepper sauce at the table instead, so everyone can add just the right amount to satisfy his or her taste buds.

1. Mix all ingredients except okra, rice and pepper sauce in 3 1/2- to 6-quart slow cooker.

2. Cover and cook on low heat setting 7 to 8 hours or until chicken is no longer pink in center.

3. Stir in okra. Cover and cook on low heat setting 20 minutes.

4. Spoon rice into individual soup bowls; top with gumbo. Serve with pepper sauce.

1 Serving: Calories 270 (Calories from Fat 80); Fat 9g (Saturated 3g); Cholesterol 35mg; Sodium 1750mg; Carbohydrate 35g (Dietary Fiber 3g); Protein 15g

% Daily Value: Vitamin A 24%; Vitamin C 14%; Calcium 10%; Iron 14%

Diet Exchanges: 2 Starch, 1 Lean Meat, 1 Vegetable, 1 Fat

Fresh Vegetable-Beef Barley Soup

■ *10 servings* ■

Crowd
SIZE

SLOW COOKER:
3 1/2- to 6-quart

PREP TIME:
20 minutes

COOK TIME:
Low 8 to 9 hours
High 4 to 5 hours

Betty's Success Tip

Select lean stew meat, or trim the extra fat before adding the beef to the soup. Trimming will take a little bit of time, but the result will be worth it since you won't have to spend time later skimming off fat.

Ingredient Substitution

If you can't find the canned diced tomatoes with garlic, use 2 cans diced tomatoes and add 1/2 teaspoon garlic powder. To save time and to make this hearty soup in the winter months, use 3/4 cup frozen cut green beans and 2/3 cup frozen whole kernel corn. Rinse the frozen vegetables under cold running water to separate and partially thaw them before adding to the soup.

Finishing Touch

Top this soup with a handful of herb-flavored croutons and a little shredded Parmesan cheese. Bursting with big, juicy chunks of meat, hearty barley and yummy vegetables, this soup is a meal in itself!

1 1/2 pounds beef stew meat

1 small bell pepper, chopped (1/2 cup)

3/4 cup 1-inch pieces green beans

3/4 cup chopped onion

2/3 cup uncooked barley

2/3 cup fresh whole kernel corn

1 1/2 cups water

1 teaspoon salt

1 teaspoon chopped fresh or 1/2 teaspoon dried thyme leaves

1/4 teaspoon pepper

2 cans (14 1/2 ounces each) ready-to-serve beef broth

2 cans (14 1/2 ounces each) diced tomatoes with garlic, undrained

1 can (8 ounces) tomato sauce

1. Mix all ingredients in 3 1/2- to 6-quart slow cooker.

2. Cover and cook on low heat setting 8 to 9 hours (or high heat setting 4 to 5 hours) or until vegetables and barley are tender.

1 Serving: Calories 200 (Calories from Fat 65); Fat 7g (Saturated 3g); Cholesterol 35mg; Sodium 1000mg; Carbohydrate 22g (Dietary Fiber 4g); Protein 16g

% Daily Value: Vitamin A 6%; Vitamin C 16%; Calcium 4%; Iron 14%

Diet Exchanges: 1 Starch, 1 1/2 Medium-Fat Meat, 1 Vegetable

Savory Cabbage and Pork Soup

■ 8 servings ■

SLOW COOKER:
3 1/2- to 6-quart

PREP TIME:
20 minutes

COOK TIME:
Low 8 to 9 hours
High 4 to 5 hours

Betty's Success Tip

Trimming the extra fat from the pork before cutting into pieces will give you a soup that is rich in flavor but not in fat.

Ingredient Substitution

If you like a slightly thicker soup, use two 14 1/2-ounce cans of ready-to-serve chicken broth instead of the water and bouillon cubes. If beef is your preference, use a pound of lean beef stew meat, cut into 1-inch pieces, and beef bouillon or broth instead of the pork and chicken broth.

Finishing Touch

Top each serving with a dollop of sour cream for a nice touch of creamy flavor.

1 pound boneless country-style pork ribs, cut into 1-inch pieces

4 medium carrots, cut into 1/4-inch slices (2 cups)

2 medium stalks celery, chopped (1 cup)

1 medium potato, peeled and cut into 1/2 × 1/4-inch pieces

1 medium onion, chopped (1/2 cup)

4 cups chopped cabbage (about 1 medium head)

1/4 cup packed brown sugar

4 cups water

1 teaspoon crushed red pepper

1/2 teaspoon salt

1/2 teaspoon pepper

4 chicken bouillon cubes

1 can (28 ounces) crushed tomatoes, undrained

1. Mix all ingredients in 3 1/2- to 6-quart slow cooker.

2. Cover and cook on low heat setting 8 to 9 hours (or high heat setting 4 to 5 hours) or until pork and vegetables are tender.

1 Serving: Calories 215 (Calories from Fat 65); Fat 7g (Saturated 2g); Cholesterol 35mg; Sodium 920mg; Carbohydrate 21g (Dietary Fiber 4g); Protein 14g

% Daily Value: Vitamin A 54%; Vitamin C 28%; Calcium 8%; Iron 8%

Diet Exchanges: 1 Starch, 1 High-Fat Meat, 1 Vegetable

Oriental Pork Soup

■ *6 servings* ■

SLOW COOKER:
3 1/2- to 6-quart

PREP TIME:
15 minutes

COOK TIME:
Low 7 to 9 hours
High 3 to 4 hours

FINISHING COOK TIME:
Low 1 hour

Betty's Success Tip

Julienne carrots are matchlike sticks of carrots that add an interesting shape to this soup. But to save a little time, you can cut the carrots into 1/4-inch slices.

Ingredient Substitution

Coarsely ground fresh pork is sometimes labeled "chow mein meat." If it isn't available at your store, use regular ground pork, chicken or turkey. Drained canned sliced mushrooms and bean sprouts come in handy when you don't have the fresh on hand.

Finishing Touch

Spoon a mound of hot cooked rice into each bowl of soup before serving, and sprinkle with some sliced green onion tops.

1 pound chow mein meat

2 medium carrots, cut into julienne strips (1 cup)

4 medium green onions, cut into 1-inch pieces (1/4 cup)

1 clove garlic, finely chopped

1/4 cup soy sauce

1/2 teaspoon finely chopped gingerroot

1/8 teaspoon pepper

1 can (49 1/2 ounces) ready-to-serve chicken broth

1 cup sliced mushrooms

1 cup bean sprouts

1. Cook chow mein meat in 10-inch skillet over medium heat 8 to 10 minutes, stirring occasionally, until brown; drain.

2. Mix meat and remaining ingredients except mushrooms and bean sprouts in 3 1/2- to 6-quart slow cooker.

3. Cover and cook on low heat setting 7 to 9 hours (or high heat setting 3 to 4 hours).

4. Stir in mushrooms and bean sprouts.

5. Cover and cook on low heat setting about 1 hour or until mushrooms are tender.

1 Serving: Calories 220 (Calories from Fat 115); Fat 13g (Saturated 4g); Cholesterol 50mg; Sodium 1720mg; Carbohydrate 6g (Dietary Fiber 1g); Protein 21g

% Daily Value: Vitamin A 28%; Vitamin C 4%; Calcium 4%; Iron 10%

Diet Exchanges: 3 Lean Meat, 1 Vegetable,1 Fat

Savory Lentil and Canadian Bacon Soup

■ 8 servings ■

SLOW COOKER:
3 1/2- to 6-quart

PREP TIME:
20 minutes

COOK TIME:
Low 8 to 9 hours
High 3 to 5 hours

Betty's Success Tip

Lentils are ideal for cooking in a slow cooker because they don't require soaking as do most dried beans and peas. The grayish green lentils are most familiar, but look for other colors such as white, yellow and red for something a little different.

Ingredient Substitution

Canadian-style bacon is a closer kin to ham than it is to regular bacon. It's taken from the lean, tender eye of the loin so it is also lower in fat, and it is fully cooked. If you have leftover ham, go ahead and use 1 1/2 cups of it for the package of Canadian-style bacon.

1 package (16 ounces) dried lentils (2 1/4 cups), sorted and rinsed

2 cans (14 1/2 ounces each) ready-to-serve vegetable broth

1 package (6 ounces) sliced Canadian-style bacon, coarsely chopped

2 medium carrots, cut into 1/2-inch pieces (1 cup)

1 medium potato, peeled and cut into 1/2-inch pieces (1 cup)

1 medium onion, chopped (1/2 cup)

1 medium stalk celery, cut into 1/2-inch pieces (1/2 cup)

4 cups water

1 teaspoon dried thyme leaves

1/2 teaspoon salt

1/4 teaspoon pepper

1. Mix all ingredients in 3 1/2- to 6-quart slow cooker.

2. Cover and cook on low heat setting 8 to 9 hours (or high heat setting 3 to 5 hours) or until lentils are tender. Stir well before serving.

1 Serving: Calories 200 (Calories from Fat 20); Fat 2g (Saturated 1g); Cholesterol 10mg; Sodium 880mg; Carbohydrate 39g (Dietary Fiber 13g); Protein 19g

% Daily Value: Vitamin A 30%; Vitamin C 6%; Calcium 4%; Iron 32%

Diet Exchanges: 1 Starch, 1 Lean Meat, 4 Vegetable

Italian Veal and Cannellini Bean Soup

■ 6 servings ■

SLOW COOKER:
3 1/2- to 6-quart

PREP TIME:
15 minutes

COOK TIME:
Low 8 to 10 hours
High 4 to 5 hours

FINISHING COOK TIME:
High 15 minutes

Betty's Success Tip

Use larger basil leaves to cut into thin strips. Stack some leaves of similar size, and roll them up starting at a long side. Cut the roll of leaves crosswise into thin strips, using a sharp knife.

Ingredient Substitution

This Italian-influenced soup can be made with pork instead of veal. Be sure to trim all the extra fat from the pork before cutting into 1-inch pieces. In a hurry? Use 1 1/2 teaspoons of lemon pepper seasoning in place of the grated lemon peel, salt and pepper.

1 1/2 pounds veal stew meat, cut into 1-inch pieces

3 medium stalks celery, cut into 1/4-inch slices (1 1/2 cups)

1 clove garlic, finely chopped

1 can (19 ounces) cannellini beans, rinsed and drained

1 can (14 1/2 ounces) ready-to-serve chicken broth

1 teaspoon grated lemon peel

1 tablespoon lemon juice

1 teaspoon salt

1/4 teaspoon pepper

1 medium red bell pepper, chopped (1 cup)

1/4 cup lightly packed fresh basil leaves, cut into thin strips

1. Mix all ingredients except bell pepper and basil in 3 1/2- to 6-quart slow cooker.

2. Cover and cook on low heat setting 8 to 10 hours (or high heat setting 4 to 5 hours) or until veal is tender.

3. Stir in bell pepper and basil.

4. Cover and cook on high heat setting about 15 minutes or until hot.

1 Serving: Calories 235 (Calories from Fat 45); Fat 5g (Saturated 2g); Cholesterol 70mg; Sodium 790mg; Carbohydrate 25g (Dietary Fiber 6g); Protein 28g

% Daily Value: Vitamin A 2%; Vitamin C 16%; Calcium 12%; Iron 24%

Diet Exchanges: 1 Starch, 3 Very Lean Meat, 2 Vegetable

Multi-Bean Soup

■ 12 servings ■

SLOW COOKER:
5 to 6-quart

PREP TIME:
10 minutes

COOK TIME:
High 8 to 10 hours

FINISHING COOK TIME:
High 15 minutes

Betty's Success Tip

The shredded carrots are added at the end so they don't overcook and disappear into the soup. Also, the tomatoes are added after the beans are tender because the acid in the tomatoes can prevent the beans from becoming tender during the long, slow cooking.

Ingredient Substitution

Have small amounts of various leftover dried beans in your cupboard? Mix them together to make 2 1/4 cups of beans, and use them instead of purchasing a package of bean soup mix. Or use a 16-ounce package of dried beans for the bean soup mix, but use only 8 cups of water and 3/4 teaspoon salt.

Finishing Touch

Add a secret ingredient to this soup for additional flavor and color—stir in 1 cup canned pumpkin when you add the carrots and tomatoes.

1 package (20 ounces) 15- or 16-dried bean soup mix, sorted and rinsed

1/2 pound smoked beef sausage ring, cut into 1/4-inch slices

1 large onion, chopped (1 cup)

10 cups water

1 1/2 teaspoons dried thyme leaves

1 teaspoon salt

1/2 teaspoon pepper

2 medium carrots, shredded (1 1/3 cups)

1 can (14 1/2 ounces) diced tomatoes, undrained

1. Mix all ingredients except carrots and tomatoes in 5- to 6-quart slow cooker.

2. Cover and cook on high heat setting 8 to 10 hours or until beans are tender.

3. Stir in carrots and tomatoes.

4. Cover and cook on high heat setting about 15 minutes or until hot.

1 Serving: Calories 210 (Calories from Fat 55); Fat 6g (Saturated 3g); Cholesterol 10mg; Sodium 660mg; Carbohydrate 35g (Dietary Fiber 6g); Protein 10g

% Daily Value: Vitamin A 22%; Vitamin C 10%; Calcium 4%; Iron 14%

Diet Exchanges: 2 Starch, 1/2 Lean Meat, 1 Vegetable

Easy Beans and Frank Soup

■ *6 servings* ■

SLOW COOKER:
3 1/2- to 6-quart

PREP TIME:
10 minutes

COOK TIME:
Low 6 to 8 hours
High 3 to 4 hours

1 can (28 ounces) baked beans with bacon and brown sugar sauce, undrained

1 can (11 1/2 ounces) eight-vegetable juice

6 franks or hot dogs, cut into 1-inch slices

3 medium carrots, chopped (1 1/2 cups)

1 large onion, chopped (1 cup)

1 clove garlic, finely chopped

1 teaspoon Worcestershire sauce

1. Mix all ingredients in 3 1/2- to 6-quart slow cooker.

2. Cover and cook on low heat setting 6 to 8 hours (or high heat setting 3 to 4 hours) or until carrots are tender.

1 Serving: Calories 295 (Calories from Fat 135); Fat 14g (Saturated 5g); Cholesterol 25mg; Sodium 1370mg; Carbohydrate 34g (Dietary Fiber 8g); Protein 14g

% Daily Value: Vitamin A 54%; Vitamin C 18%; Calcium 8%; Iron 16%

Diet Exchanges: 2 Starch, 1 High-Fat Meat, 1 Vegetable

Ingredient Substitution

The eight-vegetable juice adds a nice spicy flavor to this easy-to-make soup. For an all-family-appeal soup, however, you may want to use tomato juice instead of the eight-vegetable juice.

Serving Suggestion

For a super-easy and nutritious meal, serve this protein-packed soup with crisp carrot and celery sticks, and pass a bowl of bright red apples for dessert.

Finishing Touch

Add a little fun by sprinkling shredded mozzarella cheese on top of each bowl of hot soup. The kids will love the way it "strings" when they spoon into it. Or top with a slice of process American cheese or some shredded Cheddar cheese—it won't string, but it will add flavor.

Lima Bean and Kielbasa Soup

■ 12 servings ■

Crowd
SIZE

SLOW COOKER:
5 to 6-quart

PREP TIME:
15 minutes

COOK TIME:
High 10 to 12 hours

FINISHING COOK TIME:
15 minutes

Betty's Success Tip

Kielbasa is a smoked sausage that is usually made of pork but sometimes has beef added. "Kielbasa," "kielbasy" or "Polish sausage" are all names for this flavorful sausage. Use turkey kielbasa for a lower-fat soup.

Ingredient Substitution

You can used other dried beans for the limas, such as great Northern, navy, kidney or cannellini beans, and the cooking time will not change. Or use 2 cups of mixed dried beans by mixing different beans together to add a variety of shapes and color to the soup.

Serving Suggestion

This recipe makes a big batch. Enjoy a meal now and freeze the remaining soup for later. If you freeze it in an airtight container, it will keep up to a month. When your mouth is watering for kielbasa and bean soup, just thaw it in the refrigerator and heat it.

1 package (16 ounces) dried lima beans, sorted and rinsed

1 pound kielbasa sausage, cut into 1/4-inch slices

2 medium carrots, cut into 1/4-inch slices (1 cup)

2 medium stalks celery, cut into 1/4-inch slices (1 cup)

1 large onion, chopped (1 cup)

2 cloves garlic, finely chopped

6 cups water

1 teaspoon salt

1/2 teaspoon pepper

1 can (14 1/2 ounces) diced tomatoes, undrained

1. Mix all ingredients except tomatoes in 5- to 6-quart slow cooker.

2. Cover and cook on high heat setting 10 to 12 hours or until beans are tender.

3. Stir in tomatoes.

4. Cover and cook on high heat setting about 15 minutes or until hot.

1 Serving: Calories 215 (Calories from Fat 100); Fat 11g (Saturated 4g); Cholesterol 20mg; Sodium 650mg; Carbohydrate 24g (Dietary Fiber 7g); Protein 12g

% Daily Value: Vitamin A 18%; Vitamin C 6%; Calcium 4%; Iron 16%

Diet Exchanges: 1 Starch, 1 High-Fat Meat, 2 Vegetable

Squash and Apple Bisque

■ 8 servings ■

SLOW COOKER:
3 1/2- to 6-quart

PREP TIME:
15 minutes

COOK TIME:
Low 8 to 10 hours
High 3 to 5 hours

FINISHING COOK TIME:
Low 15 minutes

1 butternut squash (2 pounds), peeled and cubed

1 medium onion, chopped (1/2 cup)

1 can (14 1/2 ounces) ready-to-serve chicken broth

2 cups applesauce

1/2 teaspoon ground ginger

1/4 teaspoon salt

1 cup sour cream

1. Mix all ingredients except sour cream in 3 1/2- to 6-quart slow cooker.

2. Cover and cook on low heat setting 8 to 10 hours (or high heat setting 3 to 5 hours) or until squash is tender.

3. Place one-third to one-half of the mixture at a time in blender or food processor. Cover and blend on high speed until smooth. Return mixture to cooker.

4. Stir in sour cream. Cover and cook on low heat setting 15 minutes or just until soup is hot; stir.

5. Garnish each serving with a dollop of sour cream.

1 Serving: Calories 140 (Calories from Fat 55); Fat 6g (Saturated 4g); Cholesterol 20mg; Sodium 330mg; Carbohydrate 19g (Dietary Fiber 2g); Protein 3g

% Daily Value: Vitamin A 70%; Vitamin C 12%; Calcium 6%; Iron 4%

Diet Exchanges: 1 Starch, 1 Vegetable, 1 Fat

Betty's Success Tip

Sour cream will break down and curdle if it is heated too long or becomes too hot. After adding the cold sour cream, cook the bisque just long enough for it to reheat. If you use reduced-fat sour cream, add it the same way.

Serving Suggestion

For a delightful taste treat, serve this bisque thoroughly chilled. Garnish with thin slices of Granny Smith apples and a sprinkling of finely chopped crystallized ginger.

Finishing Touch

Spoon a dollop of sour cream on top of each serving, then swirl slightly into the soup with the tip of a knife. For a touch of crunch and color, sprinkle with poppy seed or chopped pecans.

Squash and Apple Bisque ➤

Potato and Double Corn Chowder

■ *6 servings* ■

SLOW COOKER:
3 1/2- to 6-quart

PREP TIME:
15 minutes

COOK TIME:
Low 6 to 8 hours
High 3 to 4 hours

Ingredient Substitution

A great way to use leftover cut-up cooked turkey or chicken is to add it to this chowder for a hearty one-dish meal. Or use cut-up fully cooked ham instead of cooking and crumbling bacon.

Finishing Touch

The bacon adds that good smoky flavor, but it does lose its crispness when added at the beginning. If you like the crisp texture of bacon, stir the bacon in at the end of the cooking instead. Also, sprinkle the chowder with some chopped fresh parsley for added color.

1 bag (16 ounces) frozen hash brown potatoes, thawed (4 cups)

1 can (15 1/4 ounces) whole kernel corn, undrained

1 can (14 3/4 ounces) cream-style corn

1 can (12 ounces) evaporated milk

1 medium onion, chopped (1/2 cup)

8 slices bacon, cooked and crumbled

1/2 teaspoon salt

1/2 teaspoon Worcestershire sauce

1/4 teaspoon pepper

1. Mix all ingredients in 3 1/2- to 6-quart slow cooker.

2. Cover and cook on low heat setting 6 to 8 hours (or high heat setting 3 to 4 hours) to develop flavors.

1 Serving: Calories 305 (Calories from Fat 65); Fat 7g (Saturated 2g); Cholesterol 12mg; Sodium 1040mg; Carbohydrate 55g (Dietary Fiber 5g); Protein 11g

% Daily Value: Vitamin A 12%; Vitamin C 18%; Calcium 10%; Iron 10%

Diet Exchanges: 3 Starch, 2 Vegetable, 1 Fat

Peppery Fish Chowder with Rice

▪ *10 servings* ▪

SLOW COOKER:
3 1/2- to 6-quart

PREP TIME:
15 minutes

COOK TIME:
Low 7 to 9 hours
High 3 to 4 hours

FINISHING COOK TIME:
High 30 to 45 minutes

Betty's Success Tip

Cutting the fish into 1-inch pieces will be a snap if you use fish steaks that are 1 inch thick or use thicker cuts of fish fillets. Any firm-fleshed fish, such as halibut, haddock, swordfish, pollack, tuna or red snapper, works well in this soup. If fish is frozen, thaw it in the refrigerator or under cold running water before cutting it into pieces and adding it to the soup.

Ingredient Substitution

The red cayenne pepper in this chowder packs a little punch, but if you prefer a chowder that's a little more tame, use black pepper instead. If you like really fiery chowder, pass a bottle of red pepper sauce at the table!

2 medium stalks celery, chopped (1 cup)

1 medium bell pepper, chopped (1 cup)

1 medium onion, chopped (1/2 cup)

2 cloves garlic, finely chopped

2 cans (14 1/2 ounces each) diced tomatoes, undrained

1/2 cup uncooked instant rice

2 cups eight-vegetable juice

1 cup dry white wine or vegetable broth

1 tablespoon Worcestershire sauce

1 teaspoon salt

1/4 teaspoon ground red pepper (cayenne)

1 pound firm-fleshed fish steak, cut into 1-inch pieces

3 tablespoons chopped fresh parsley

1. Mix all ingredients except fish and parsley in 3 1/2- to 6-quart slow cooker.

2. Cover and cook on low heat setting 7 to 9 hours (or high heat setting 3 to 4 hours) or until rice is tender.

3. Stir in fish and parsley.

4. Cover and cook on high heat setting 30 to 45 minutes or until fish flakes easily with fork.

1 Serving: Calories 90 (Calories from Fat 10); Fat 1g (Saturated 0g); Cholesterol 20mg; Sodium 540mg; Carbohydrate 13g (Dietary Fiber 2g); Protein 9g

% Daily Value: Vitamin A 12%; Vitamin C 32%; Calcium 4%; Iron 6%

Diet Exchanges: 1 Starch, 1 Very Lean Meat

Chicken Stew with Pepper and Pineapple

4 servings

SLOW COOKER:
3 1/2- to 6-quart

PREP TIME:
20 minutes

COOK TIME:
Low 7 to 8 hours
High 3 to 4 hours

FINISHING COOK TIME:
High 15 minutes

Ingredient Substitution

If you don't have fresh gingerroot, no problem! Just use 1 teaspoon ground ginger in place of it.

Finishing Touch

To be sure you get every last drop of the yummy gingery-flavored sauce, spoon the stew over hot cooked rice. To turn a great stew into an extra-special stew, just sprinkle with sliced green onions and toasted coconut or chopped peanuts or cashews.

1 pound skinless, boneless chicken breasts, cut into 1 1/2-inch pieces

4 medium carrots, cut into 1-inch pieces

1/2 cup chicken broth

2 tablespoons finely chopped gingerroot

1 tablespoon packed brown sugar

2 tablespoons soy sauce

1/2 teaspoon ground allspice

1/2 teaspoon red pepper sauce

1 can (8 ounces) pineapple chunks in juice, drained and juice reserved

1 tablespoon cornstarch

1 medium bell pepper, cut into 1-inch pieces

1. Mix all ingredients except pineapple, cornstarch and bell pepper in 3 1/2- to 6-quart slow cooker.

2. Cover and cook on low heat setting 7 to 8 hours (or high heat setting 3 to 4 hours) or until vegetables are tender and chicken is no longer pink in center.

3. Mix reserved pineapple juice and cornstarch until smooth; gradually stir into chicken mixture. Stir in pineapple and bell pepper.

4. Cover and cook on high heat setting about 15 minutes or until slightly thickened.

1 Serving: Calories 225 (Calories from Fat 30); Fat 4g (Saturated 1g); Cholesterol 70mg; Sodium 690mg; Carbohydrate 24g (Dietary Fiber 3g); Protein 27g

% Daily Value: Vitamin A 96%; Vitamin C 32%; Calcium 4%; Iron 10%

Diet Exchanges: 3 1/2 Very Lean Meat, 2 Vegetable, 1 Fruit

Brunswick Stew

■ 10 servings ■

Crowd
S I Z E

SLOW COOKER:
3 1/2- to 6-quart

PREP TIME:
20 minutes

COOK TIME:
Low 8 to 10 hours
High 3 to 4 hours

Betty's Success Tip

Traditionally, Brunswick Stew is made with whole kernel corn, but we like the creaminess that the cream-style corn gives this southern favorite. Be sure to cut the potatoes into 1/2-inch pieces, so they will be tender when the stew is done cooking.

Ingredient Substitution

Lima is the popular bean for this stew, but a drained 16-ounce can of butter beans gives the same great results.

Serving Suggestion

Brunswick Stew is a popular classic from Virginia's Brunswick County, hence its name. This hearty stew originally was made of squirrel and onion, but today chicken is the more popular meat of choice. Warm baking powder biscuits slathered with butter, another southern favorite, will be all you need for a satisfying meal.

1 1/2 pounds skinless, boneless chicken breasts, cut into 1-inch pieces

3 medium potatoes, cut into 1/2-inch pieces

1 medium onion, chopped (1/2 cup)

1 can (28 ounces) crushed tomatoes, undrained

1 can (15 to 16 ounces) lima beans, rinsed and drained

1 can (14 3/4 ounces) cream-style corn

1 tablespoon Worcestershire sauce

3/4 teaspoon salt

1/2 teaspoon dried marjoram leaves

8 slices bacon, cooked and crumbled

1/4 teaspoon red pepper sauce

1. Mix all ingredients except bacon and pepper sauce in 3 1/2- to 6-quart slow cooker.

2. Cover and cook on low heat setting 8 to 10 hours (or high heat setting 3 to 4 hours) or until potatoes are tender.

3. Stir in bacon and pepper sauce.

1 Serving: Calories 250 (Calories from Fat 55); Fat 6g (Saturated 2g); Cholesterol 50mg; Sodium 630mg; Carbohydrate 31g (Dietary Fiber 6g); Protein 24g

% Daily Value: Vitamin A 6%; Vitamin C 16%; Calcium 4%; Iron 16%

Diet Exchanges: 1 Starch, 2 Lean Meat, 3 Vegetable

Sausage Gumbo

8 servings

SLOW COOKER:
3 1/2- to 6-quart

PREP TIME:
15 minutes

COOK TIME:
Low 7 to 9 hours
High 3 to 4 hours

FINISHING COOK TIME:
High 30 minutes

Betty's Success Tip

Okra not only adds flavor, but as it cooks it helps to thicken the gumbo sauce. It's a popular vegetable throughout the South and is a signature ingredient for gumbos. In fact, the name gumbo is a derivation of the African word for "okra." This vegetable was brought to the South from Africa.

Ingredient Substitution

Some gumbos are made with a variety of meats instead of just sausage. Cut 1/2 pound of skinless, boneless chicken breasts or thighs, beef round steak or ham into 1/2-inch pieces, and add with 1/2 pound of sliced sausage. Or use a little of each to equal a pound of meat.

Finishing Touch

Adding greens to your gumbo is a symbol for good luck. Place about 4 cups of fresh spinach on top of the cooked gumbo. Cover the cooker and let it stand about 10 minutes or until the spinach is wilted. Stir the spinach into the gumbo before serving.

1 pound fully cooked smoked sausage, cut into 1/2-inch slices

1 medium green bell pepper, chopped (1 cup)

1 medium onion, chopped (1/2 cup)

2 cloves garlic, finely chopped

1 can (28 ounces) crushed tomatoes, undrained

1 tablespoon Worcestershire sauce

1/4 teaspoon salt

1/4 teaspoon pepper

1 package (10 ounces) frozen sliced okra, thawed and drained

1 tablespoon white vinegar

1/4 to 1/2 teaspoon red pepper sauce

4 cups hot cooked rice, for serving

1. Mix sausage, bell pepper, onion, garlic, tomatoes, Worcestershire sauce, salt and pepper in 3 1/2- to 6-quart slow cooker.

2. Cover and cook on low heat setting 7 to 9 hours (or high heat setting 3 to 4 hours) or until vegetables are tender.

3. Stir in okra, vinegar and pepper sauce.

4. Cover and cook on high heat setting about 30 minutes or until slightly thickened.

5. Serve gumbo over rice.

1 Serving: Calories 305 (Calories from Fat 145); Fat 16g (Saturated 6g); Cholesterol 30mg; Sodium 820mg; Carbohydrate 32g (Dietary Fiber 3g); Protein 11g

% Daily Value: Vitamin A 8%; Vitamin C 26%; Calcium 8%; Iron 14%

Diet Exchanges: 2 Starch, 1 High-Fat Meat, 1 Fat

Jambalaya

■ *8 servings* ■

SLOW COOKER:
3 1/2- to 6-quart

PREP TIME:
20 minutes

COOK TIME:
Low 7 to 8 hours
High 3 to 4 hours

FINISHING COOK TIME:
Low 1 hour

Ingredient Substitution

Andouille sausage, which is a spicy, heavily smoked sausage, is the traditional sausage for jambalaya. Any sausage will taste good, however, and a smoked turkey sausage will add flavor but not as much fat as regular sausage. Have leftover ham in the refrigerator? Use the same amount of ham for the sausage.

Serving Suggestion

Here's a fun way of serving rice. Spray the inside of a 1/2-cup measuring cup with cooking spray. For each serving, press the hot rice into the cup. Place the cup upside down in the bottom of a bowl and unmold the rice. Spoon the jambalaya around the mound of rice. Serve with warm crusty bread.

Finishing Touch

If you prefer more "heat," sprinkle additional red pepper sauce on this Cajun favorite just before serving. If you want to use fresh parsley and thyme, add them with the shrimp so the flavor isn't lost during the long cooking.

1 large onion, chopped (1 cup)

1 medium green bell pepper, chopped (1 cup)

2 medium stalks celery, chopped (1 cup)

3 cloves garlic, finely chopped

1 can (28 ounces) diced tomatoes, undrained

2 cups chopped fully cooked smoked sausage

1 tablespoon parsley flakes

1/2 teaspoon dried thyme leaves

1/2 teaspoon salt

1/4 teaspoon pepper

1/4 teaspoon red pepper sauce

3/4 pound uncooked peeled deveined medium shrimp, thawed if frozen

4 cups hot cooked rice, for serving

1. Mix all ingredients except shrimp and rice in 3 1/2- to 6-quart slow cooker.

2. Cover and cook on low heat setting 7 to 8 hours (or high heat setting 3 to 4 hours) or until vegetables are tender.

3. Stir in shrimp. Cover and cook on low heat setting about 1 hour or until shrimp are pink and firm.

4. Serve jambalaya with rice.

1 Serving: Calories 255 (Calories from Fat 90); Fat 10g (Saturated 4g); Cholesterol 60mg; Sodium 710mg; Carbohydrate 31g (Dietary Fiber 2g); Protein 12g

% Daily Value: Vitamin A 8%; Vitamin C 28%; Calcium 6%; Iron 16%

Diet Exchanges: 2 Starch, 1 High-Fat Meat

Beef Stew with Sun-Dried Tomatoes

■ *6 servings* ■

SLOW COOKER:
3 1/2- to 6-quart

PREP TIME:
20 minutes

COOK TIME:
Low 8 to 9 hours
High 3 to 5 hours

FINISHING COOK TIME:
High 10 to 15 minutes

1 cup sun-dried tomatoes (not oil-packed)

1 1/2 pounds beef stew meat

12 medium new potatoes (1 1/2 pounds), cut in half

1 medium onion, cut into 8 wedges

1 bag (8 ounces) baby-cut carrots (about 30)

2 cups water

1 1/2 teaspoons seasoned salt

1 bay leaf

1/4 cup cold water

2 tablespoons all-purpose flour

1. Soak tomatoes in water as directed on package; drain and coarsely chop.

2. Mix tomatoes and remaining ingredients except 1/4 cup water and the flour in 3 1/2- to 6-quart slow cooker.

3. Cover and cook on low heat setting 8 to 9 hours (or high heat setting 3 to 5 hours) or until beef and vegetables are tender.

4. Mix 1/4 cup water and the flour; gradually stir into beef mixture.

5. Cover and cook on high heat setting 10 to 15 minutes or until slightly thickened. Remove bay leaf.

1 Serving: Calories 310 (Calories from Fat 100); Fat 11g (Saturated 4g); Cholesterol 60mg; Sodium 600mg; Carbohydrate 34g (Dietary Fiber 5g); Protein 24g

% Daily Value: Vitamin A 78%; Vitamin C 16%; Calcium 4%; Iron 24%

Diet Exchanges: 2 Starch, 2 Lean Meat, 1 Vegetable, 1/2 Fat

Betty's Success Tip

Purchased stew meat does save time, but other cuts of beef also work well for this stew. Try chuck, tip or top or bottom round steak. Get a 1-inch-thick piece of boneless steak, trim the extra fat and cut the steak into 1-inch pieces.

Ingredient Substitution

Sun-dried tomatoes, or dried-tomatoes, add a nice concentrated tomato flavor to the stew. When fresh tomatoes are plentiful, you can add 2 cups chopped fresh tomatoes with the flour mixture instead of using the dried tomatoes.

Finishing Touch

Serve stew in bowls, and sprinkle each serving with crumbled crisply cooked bacon and chopped fresh parsley.

Burgundy Stew with Herb Dumplings

■ *8 servings* ■

SLOW COOKER:
3 1/2- to 6-quart

PREP TIME:
25 minutes

COOK TIME:
Low 8 to 10 hours
High 4 to 5 hours

FINISHING COOK TIME:
High 25 to 35 minutes

Betty's Success Tip

To make fluffy dumplings, drop the dumpling dough on the stew pieces rather than directly into the liquid. The dumplings will steam rather than settle into the liquid and become soggy. Also, be sure the stew is piping hot, so the dumplings will start to cook from the steam right away and become fluffy.

Ingredient Substitution

Save time cleaning and slicing carrots, and use 2 cups of baby-cut carrots instead. Keeping a bag of ready-to-eat baby-cut carrots in the refrigerator is handy for nibbling on or to have ready to put into soups or stews.

Serving Suggestion

Want to save some time by not making the dumplings? Instead, just serve the stew in bowls with big chunks of crusty Italian bread for dipping into the stew and soaking up all the delicious wine-flavored broth.

2 pounds beef boneless bottom or top round, cut into 1-inch pieces

4 medium carrots, cut into 1/4-inch slices (2 cups)

2 medium stalks celery, sliced (1 cup)

2 medium onions, sliced

1 can (14 1/2 ounces) diced tomatoes, undrained

1 can (8 ounces) sliced mushrooms, drained

3/4 cup dry red wine or beef broth

1 1/2 teaspoons salt

1 teaspoon dried thyme leaves

1 teaspoon ground mustard (dry)

1/4 teaspoon pepper

1/4 cup water

3 tablespoons all-purpose flour

Herb Dumplings (below)

1. Mix all ingredients except water, flour and Herb Dumplings in 3 1/2- to 6-quart slow cooker.

2. Cover and cook on low heat setting 8 to 10 hours (or high heat setting 4 to 5 hours) or until vegetables and beef are tender. Mix water and flour; gradually stir into beef mixture.

3. Prepare Herb Dumplings. Drop dough by spoonfuls onto hot beef mixture. Cover and cook on high heat setting 25 to 35 minutes or until toothpick inserted in center of dumplings comes out clean.

Herb Dumplings

Mix 1 1/2 cups Bisquick® Original baking mix, 1/2 teaspoon dried thyme leaves, and 1/4 teaspoon dried sage leaves, crumbled. Stir in 1/2 cup milk just until baking mix is moistened.

1 Serving: Calories 255 (Calories from Fat 65); Fat 7g (Saturated 2g); Cholesterol 55mg; Sodium 1030mg; Carbohydrate26g (Dietary Fiber 3g); Protein 25g

% Daily Value: Vitamin A 50%; Vitamin C 10%; Calcium 10%; Iron 20%

Diet Exchanges: 1 Starch, 2 Lean Meat, 2 Vegetable

Irish Stew

■ 8 servings ■

SLOW COOKER:
3 1/2- to 6-quart

PREP TIME:
15 minutes

COOK TIME:
Low 8 to 10 hours
High 3 to 5 hours

Ingredient Substitution

This stew also can be made with 2 pounds of lean beef stew meat instead of the lamb. It is so easy, you will want to make it an everyday favorite.

Serving Suggestion

Plan to serve this stew on a Saturday or Sunday evening. Take the time to bake a loaf of Irish soda bread, using your favorite recipe. Complete the meal with tall glasses of full-bodied stout beer. This meal is so good, it will put you in the mood to dance a jig!

Finishing Touch

Like green peas in your Irish stew? Thaw a cup of frozen green peas, or rinse them under cold running water until separated and thawed. Stir them into the stew after you have skimmed off the fat, and let the heat of the stew warm the peas.

2 pounds lean lamb stew meat

6 medium potatoes (2 pounds), cut into 1/2-inch slices

3 medium onions, sliced

1 teaspoon salt

1/4 teaspoon pepper

1 teaspoon dried thyme leaves

1 can (14 1/2 ounces) ready-to-serve beef broth

Chopped fresh parsley, if desired

1. Layer half each of the lamb, potatoes and onions in 3 1/2- to 6-quart slow cooker. Sprinkle with half each of the salt, pepper and thyme. Repeat layers and sprinkle with remaining seasonings. Pour broth over top.

2. Cover and cook on low heat setting 8 to 10 hours (or high heat setting 3 to 5 hours) or until lamb and vegetables are tender.

3. Skim fat from stew. Sprinkle parsley over stew.

1 Serving: Calories 250 (Calories from Fat 65); Fat 7g (Saturated 2g); Cholesterol 60mg; Sodium 590mg; Carbohydrate 27g (Dietary Fiber 3g); Protein 23g

% Daily Value: Vitamin A 0%; Vitamin C 12%; Calcium 2%; Iron 16%

Diet Exchanges: 1 Starch, 2 Lean Meat, 2 Vegetable

Hearty Pork Stew

■ *6 servings* ■

SLOW COOKER:
3 1/2- to 6-quart
PREP TIME:
25 minutes
COOK TIME:
Low 6 to 7 hours
High 3 to 4 hours
FINISHING COOK TIME:
High 30 to 45 minutes

Betty's Success Tip

Chicken broth is available in an aseptic box that is handy to use. It has an easy-to-open pour spout, and any leftover broth can be stored in the box in the refrigerator. Four cups of chicken broth or broth made from bouillon cubes or granules can be used in place of the box of broth.

Ingredient Substitution

Parsnips, that root vegetable that looks like a creamy white carrot, have a slightly sweet flavor that goes nicely with pork. However, instead of the parsnips, two more sliced carrots can be used and the stew will be just as colorful and tasty.

1 1/2 pounds pork boneless loin, cut into 1-inch cubes

3 medium carrots, cut into 1/4-inch slices (1 1/2 cups)

1 medium onion, chopped (1/2 cup)

1 box (32 ounces) ready-to-serve chicken broth

2 cups 1/2-inch diced peeled parsnips

1 1/2 cups 1-inch cubes peeled butternut squash

1/2 teaspoon salt

1/2 teaspoon pepper

3 tablespoons all-purpose flour

3 tablespoons margarine or butter, softened

1. Mix all ingredients except flour and margarine in 3 1/2- to 6-quart slow cooker.

2. Cover and cook on low heat setting 6 to 7 hours (or high heat setting 3 to 4 hours) or until pork is no longer pink and vegetables are tender.

3. Mix flour and margarine. Gently stir flour mixture, 1 spoonful at a time, into pork mixture until blended.

4. Cover and cook on high heat setting 30 to 45 minutes, stirring occasionally, until thickened.

1 Serving: Calories 275 (Calories from Fat 115); Fat 13g (Saturated 4g); Cholesterol 50mg; Sodium 1010mg; Carbohydrate 21g (Dietary Fiber 4g); Protein 23g

% Daily Value: Vitamin A 80%; Vitamin C 12%; Calcium 6%; Iron 10%

Diet Exchanges: 1 Starch, 2 1/2 Medium-Fat Meat, 1 Vegetable

Venison Stew

■ *8 servings* ■

SLOW COOKER:
3 1/2- to 6-quart

PREP TIME:
20 minutes

COOK TIME:
Low 8 to 10 hours

FINISHING COOK TIME:
High 30 minutes

Ingredient Substitution

If you aren't "game" for venison, you still can enjoy this savory, sweet-sour-flavored stew by using the same amount of lean beef stew meat. If the chunks of beef are large, cut them into 1-inch pieces.

Serving Suggestion

Be sure to serve plenty of hearty whole-grain bread with this stew so everyone can sop up every last drop of the wonderful gravy in the bottom of the bowl!

2 pounds venison, cut into 1-inch pieces

2 medium onions, cut into 1/2-inch slices

1 pound small red potatoes, cut into 1/4-inch slices

2 medium apples, cut into 1/2-inch slices

1 bay leaf

1 can (10 1/2 ounces) condensed beef broth

1 cup red Burgundy wine or beef broth

1/2 cup Worcestershire sauce

1/2 cup packed brown sugar

1/8 teaspoon pepper

2 cloves garlic, finely chopped

1/4 cup all-purpose flour

1/4 cup water

1. Layer venison, onions, potatoes, apples and bay leaf in 31/2- to 6-quart slow cooker. Mix wine or broth, Worcestershire sauce, brown sugar, pepper and garlic; pour into cooker.

2. Cover and cook on low heat setting 8 to 10 hours or until venison is tender.

3. Mix flour and water; stir into venison mixture. Cover and cook on high heat setting about 30 minutes or until slightly thickened. Remove bay leaf.

1 Serving: Calories 285 (Calories from Fat 25); Fat 3g (Saturated 1g); Cholesterol 95mg; Sodium 310mg; Carbohydrate 39g (Dietary Fiber 3g); Protein 28g

% Daily Value: Vitamin A 0%; Vitamin C 10%; Calcium 4%; Iron 32%

Diet Exchanges: 1 Starch, 3 Very Lean Meat, 2 Vegetable, 1 Fruit

Turkey and Brown Rice Chili

■ *6 servings* ■

Slow Cooker:
3 1/2- to 6-quart

Prep Time:
15 minutes

Cook Time:
Low 8 to 10 hours
High 4 to 5 hours

Finishing Cook Time:
High 15 minutes

Betty's Success Tip

This is a lower-fat chili because it is made with ground turkey breast. Make sure that you are buying ground turkey breast and not regular ground turkey, which includes both light and dark meat and will be higher in fat.

Ingredient Substitution

Have ground beef in the freezer? Use it instead of the turkey, and you won't need the oil to cook it in. Stir in either brown or white rice to finish the chili.

Finishing Touch

Enjoy this chili topped with your favorite salsa and corn chips. Like cilantro? Stir a couple of tablespoons of chopped fresh cilantro into the chili before serving.

1 tablespoon vegetable oil

3/4 pound ground turkey breast

1 large onion, chopped (1 cup)

2 cans (14 1/2 ounces each) diced tomatoes, undrained

1 can (15 or 16 ounces) chili beans in sauce, undrained

1 can (4 ounces) chopped green chilies, drained

1/2 cup water

1 tablespoon sugar

2 teaspoons chili powder

1 teaspoon ground cumin

1/2 teaspoon salt

2 cups cooked brown rice

1. Heat oil in 12-inch skillet over medium heat. Cook turkey and onion in oil, stirring frequently, until turkey is no longer pink; drain.

2. Mix turkey mixture and remaining ingredients except rice in 3 1/2- to 6-quart slow cooker.

3. Cover and cook on low heat setting 8 to 10 hours (or high heat setting 4 to 5 hours).

4. Stir in rice.

5. Cover and cook on high heat setting about 15 minutes or until rice is hot.

1 Serving: Calories 235 (Calories from Fat 30); Fat 4g (Saturated 1g); Cholesterol 40mg; Sodium 980mg; Carbohydrate 37g (Dietary Fiber 6g); Protein 20g

% Daily Value: Vitamin A 14%; Vitamin C 34%; Calcium 8%; Iron 20%

Diet Exchanges: 2 Starch, 2 Very Lean Meat, 1 Vegetable

Vegetarian Chili with Baked Tortilla Strips

▪ *6 servings* ▪

SLOW COOKER:
3 1/2- to 6-quart

PREP TIME:
15 minutes

COOK TIME:
Low 5 to 6 hours

Ingredient Substitution

Use any canned beans that you have on hand for the pinto or kidney beans. For variety, try great northern, black, garbanzo or lima beans, as well as black-eyed peas.

Serving Suggestion

This bean-packed chili is great served over hot cooked brown or white rice to make a heartier meatless meal. You decide if you want the tortilla strips on top.

Finishing Touch

For a cool zing, mix a tablespoon or two of fresh lime juice into 1 cup of sour cream to spoon on top of the chili. Sprinkle with chopped fresh cilantro or sliced green onions.

Baked Tortilla Strips (below)

1 can (15 or 16 ounces) spicy chili beans in sauce, undrained

1 can (15 to 16 ounces) pinto beans, undrained

1 can (15 to 16 ounces) dark red kidney beans, drained

1 can (14 1/2 ounces) chili-style chunky tomatoes, undrained

1 large onion, chopped (1 cup)

2 to 3 teaspoons chili powder

1/8 teaspoon ground red pepper (cayenne)

1. Prepare Baked Tortilla Strips.

2. Mix remaining ingredients in 3 1/2- to 6-quart slow cooker.

3. Cover and cook on low heat setting 5 to 6 hours or until flavors have blended.

4. Stir well before serving. Spoon chili over tortilla strips, or sprinkle tortilla strips on top.

Baked Tortilla Strips

Heat oven to 400°. Cut 2 flour tortillas (8 inches in diameter) in half; cut each half crosswise into 1/2-inch strips. Place in single layer on ungreased cookie sheet. Bake 10 to 12 minutes or until strips are crisp and edges are light brown.

1 Serving: Calories 220 (Calories from Fat 20); Fat 2g (Saturated 0g); Cholesterol 0mg; Sodium 880mg; Carbohydrate 48g (Dietary Fiber 12g); Protein 14g

% Daily Value: Vitamin A 10%; Vitamin C 16%; Calcium 10%; Iron 28%

Diet Exchanges: 2 Starch, 3 Vegetable

Family Favorite Chili

■ *8 servings* ■

SLOW COOKER:
3 1/2- to 6-quart

PREP TIME:
20 minutes

COOK TIME:
Low 6 to 8 hours
High 3 to 4 hours

FINISHING COOK TIME:
High 15 to 20 minutes

Betty's Success Tip

Starting with hot cooked ground beef is safer because getting cold, uncooked ground beef to a safe temperature in a slow cooker takes too long. Also, using cooked and drained ground beef helps eliminate that extra fat and liquid that would accumulate during cooking.

Ingredient Substitution

Like a hot and spicy chili? Use a pound of ground beef and a pound of hot and spicy pork or Italian bulk sausage instead of all beef. Cook and drain the two together before adding to the cooker.

Serving Suggestion

Chili is great by itself in a bowl, and it also makes a great topper. For a Cincinnati-style treat, serve chili over hot cooked spaghetti and sprinkle with shredded Cheddar cheese and chopped onion. Kids love chili spooned on corn chips because it reminds them of a taco.

2 pounds ground beef

1 large onion, chopped (1 cup)

2 cloves garlic, finely chopped

1 can (28 ounces) diced tomatoes, undrained

1 can (15 ounces) tomato sauce

2 tablespoons chili powder

1 1/2 teaspoons ground cumin

1/2 teaspoon salt

1/2 teaspoon pepper

1 can (15 or 16 ounces) kidney or pinto beans, rinsed and drained

1. Cook beef in 12-inch skillet over medium heat, stirring occasionally, until brown; drain.

2. Mix beef and remaining ingredients except beans in 3 1/2- to 6-quart slow cooker.

3. Cover and cook on low heat setting 6 to 8 hours (or high heat setting 3 to 4 hours) or until onion is tender.

4. Stir in beans. Cover and cook on high heat setting 15 to 20 minutes or until slightly thickened.

1 Serving: Calories 335 (Calories from Fat 155); Fat 17g (Saturated 7g); Cholesterol 65mg; Sodium 820mg; Carbohydrate 24g (Dietary Fiber 6g); Protein 28g

% Daily Value: Vitamin A 18%; Vitamin C 20%; Calcium 6%; Iron 28%

Diet Exchanges: 1 Starch, 3 Medium-Fat Meat, 2 Vegetable

Chunky Pork and Beef Sausage Chili

■ 6 servings ■

SLOW COOKER:
3 1/2- to 6-quart

PREP TIME:
20 minutes

COOK TIME:
Low 8 to 10 hours
High 3 to 5 hours

Ingredient Substitution

For a "white" chili, leave out the sausage and use 2 pounds of pork. Add a can of great Northern or pinto beans instead of the black beans.

Serving Suggestion

Decided at the last minute to invite some friends over for chili? Stir in an extra can or two of your favorite beans. Each can will increase the number of servings by two.

Finishing Touch

Let everyone add his or her own special touch by passing bowls of shredded Cheddar cheese, chopped avocado, sliced jalapeño chilies, chopped onion, sliced ripe olives, chopped fresh cilantro and sour cream.

1 pound lean boneless pork, cut into 3/4-inch pieces

1/2 pound fully cooked smoked beef sausage, cut into 1/2-inch slices

1 large onion, chopped (1 cup)

2 medium stalks celery, sliced (1 cup)

2 cloves garlic, finely chopped

1 can (15 ounces) black beans, rinsed and drained

1 can (15 ounces) chunky tomato sauce

1 can (10 ounces) diced tomatoes and green chilies

1 cup water

1 1/2 teaspoons chili powder

1/2 teaspoon ground cumin

1/2 teaspoon salt

1/4 teaspoon pepper

1. Mix all ingredients in 3 1/2- to 6-quart slow cooker.

2. Cover and cook on low heat setting 8 to 10 hours (or high heat setting 3 to 5 hours) or until pork is tender.

1 Serving: Calories 380 (Calories from Fat 160); Fat 18g (Saturated 7g); Cholesterol 70mg; Sodium 1420mg; Carbohydrate 31g (Dietary Fiber 7g); Protein 30g

% Daily Value: Vitamin A 12%; Vitamin C 18%; Calcium 10%; Iron 22%

Diet Exchanges: 2 Starch, 3 Medium-Fat Meat

Meaty
Main
Dishes

◄ *Savory Pot Roast (page 59)*

Beef and Potatoes with Rosemary

■ *8 servings* ■

SLOW COOKER:
3 1/2- to 6-quart

PREP TIME:
20 minutes

COOK TIME:
Low 8 to 10 hours

Ingredient Substitution

Just run out of onions? You can add a teaspoon of onion powder with the mustard mixture to spread on the beef instead of chopping a fresh onion.

Finishing Touch

If your family likes gravy, you may want to thicken the beef juices. Skim fat from juices. Measure 1 1/2 cups of the juices from the cooker; pour into a small saucepan. Heat to boiling over medium-high heat. Shake 2 tablespoons cornstarch and 1/4 cup cold water in a tightly covered jar. Stir cornstarch mixture into beef juices. Cook about 5 minutes, stirring occasionally, until thickened.

1 pound medium red potatoes, cut into fourths

1 cup baby-cut carrots

3-pound beef boneless chuck roast

3 tablespoons Dijon mustard

2 tablespoons chopped fresh or 1 1/2 teaspoons dried rosemary leaves, crumbled

1 teaspoon chopped fresh or 1/2 teaspoon dried thyme leaves

1 teaspoon salt

1/2 teaspoon pepper

1 small onion, finely chopped (1/4 cup)

1 1/2 cups beef broth

1. Arrange potatoes and carrots in 3 1/2- to 6-quart slow cooker.

2. Trim excess fat from beef. Mix mustard, rosemary, thyme, salt and pepper; spread evenly over beef. Place beef in cooker. Sprinkle onion over beef. Pour broth evenly over beef and vegetables.

3. Cover and cook on low heat setting 8 to 10 hours or until beef and vegetables are tender.

4. Remove beef and vegetables from cooker, using slotted spoon; place on serving platter. Skim fat from beef juices in cooker if desired. Serve beef with juices.

1 Serving: Calories 250 (Calories from Fat 110); Fat 12g (Saturated 4g); Cholesterol 60mg; Sodium 550mg; Carbohydrate 14g (Dietary Fiber 2g); Protein 23g

% Daily Value: Vitamin A 24%; Vitamin C 6%; Calcium 2%; Iron 18%

Diet Exchanges: 1 Starch, 3 Lean Meat

New England Pot Roast

■ 8 servings ■

Slow Cooker:
4- to 6-quart

Prep Time:
20 minutes

Cook Time:
Low 8 to 10 hours

Betty's Success Tip

Yes, the entire jar of prepared horseradish is spread on top of the roast. The flavor of the horseradish becomes subtle during the long, slow cooking. It's our best kept secret ingredient we'd like to share with you! You can find horseradish in the refrigerator section of your supermarket.

Serving Suggestion

The great thing about serving a pot roast dinner is that everything—meat and vegetables—is included in one dish. Complete this easy meal with a good old-fashioned dessert, such as warm apple crisp, bread pudding or cherry cobbler.

3- to 3 1/2-pound beef boneless chuck roast

1 tablespoon vegetable oil

8 small potatoes, cut in half

3 cups baby-cut carrots

1 large onion, coarsely chopped (1 cup)

1 jar (5 ounces) prepared horseradish

1 teaspoon salt

1/2 teaspoon pepper

1 cup water

1. Trim excess fat from beef. Heat oil in 10-inch skillet over medium-high heat. Cook beef in oil about 10 minutes, turning occasionally, until brown on all sides.

2. Place potatoes, carrots and onions in 4- to 6-quart slow cooker. Place beef on vegetables. Mix horseradish, salt and pepper; spread evenly over beef.

3. Pour water over beef and vegetables. Cover and cook on low heat setting 8 to 10 hours or until beef and vegetables are tender.

1 Serving: Calories 345 (Calories from Fat 135); Fat 15g (Saturated 5g); Cholesterol 75mg; Sodium 390mg; Carbohydrate 30g (Dietary Fiber 4g); Protein 27g

% Daily Value: Vitamin A 70%; Vitamin C 16%; Calcium 4%; Iron 24%

Diet Exchanges: 1 Starch, 2 1/2 Medium-Fat Meat, 3 Vegetable

Savory Pot Roast

■ 6 servings ■

SLOW COOKER:
4- to 6-quart

PREP TIME:
20 minutes

COOK TIME:
Low 8 to 10 hours

FINISHING COOK TIME:
High 15 minutes

Betty's Success Tip

A quick way to mix the flour with the liquid is to use a jar. Screw the lid on tight, and shake the jar until the mixture is smooth. This is faster than trying to stir it until all the lumps of flour are dissolved.

Ingredient Substitution

If you just have tomato juice in your cupboard, go ahead and use it instead of the eight-vegetable juice. Regular-size carrots, cut into 2-inch pieces, can be used if you are out of baby-cut carrots. And a drained 4-ounce can of sliced mushrooms can be used instead of the fresh mushrooms.

Serving Suggestion

Leftover beef and vegetable sauce? Turn it into savory beef and vegetable soup for another meal. Shred the beef, and stir it into the vegetable sauce. Add enough beef broth to make it the soup consistency that you like. Just heat it, and top each serving with a sprinkle of shredded Cheddar cheese. It's a great disguise for leftovers!

2- to 2 1/2-pound beef bottom round roast

2 teaspoons olive or vegetable oil

2 or 3 medium potatoes, cut into 2-inch pieces

2 1/2 cups baby-cut carrots

2 cups sliced mushrooms (about 5 ounces)

1 medium stalk celery, sliced (1/2 cup)

1 medium onion, chopped (1/2 cup)

1 teaspoon salt

1/2 teaspoon pepper

1/2 teaspoon dried thyme leaves

1 can (14 1/2 ounces) diced tomatoes, undrained

1 can (10 1/2 ounces) condensed beef consommé or broth

1 can (5 1/2 ounces) eight-vegetable juice

1/4 cup all-purpose flour

1. Trim excess fat from beef. Heat oil in 10-inch skillet over medium-high heat. Cook beef in oil about 10 minutes, turning occasionally, until brown on all sides.

2. Place potatoes, carrots, mushrooms, celery and onion in 4- to 6-quart slow cooker. Sprinkle with salt, pepper and thyme. Place beef on vegetables. Pour tomatoes, consommé and vegetable juice over beef.

3. Cover and cook on low heat setting 8 to 10 hours or until beef and vegetables are tender.

4. Remove beef and vegetables from cooker, using slotted spoon; place on serving platter and keep warm.

5. Skim fat from beef juices in cooker if desired. Remove 1/2 cup of the juices from the cooker; mix with flour until smooth. Gradually stir flour mixture into remaining juices in cooker. Cook on high heat setting about 15 minutes or until thickened. Serve sauce with beef and vegetables.

1 Serving: Calories 270 (Calories from Fat 55); Fat 6g (Saturated 2g); Cholesterol 75mg; Sodium 880mg; Carbohydrate 26g (Dietary Fiber 4g); Protein 32g

% Daily Value: Vitamin A 90%; Vitamin C 24%; Calcium 6%; Iron 26%

Diet Exchanges: 1 Starch, 3 Lean Meat, 2 Vegetable

Caramelized Onion Pot Roast

■ 12 servings ■

SLOW COOKER:
3 1/2- to 6-quart

PREP TIME:
25 minutes

COOK TIME:
Low 8 to 10 hours

4-pound beef boneless chuck roast

1 tablespoon olive or vegetable oil

1 teaspoon salt

1/2 teaspoon pepper

6 medium onions, sliced

1 1/2 cups beef broth

3/4 cup beer

2 tablespoons packed brown sugar

3 tablespoons Dijon mustard

2 tablespoons cider vinegar

What a Great Idea. . .
for Leftovers

If you're lucky enough to have leftovers from this flavor-packed roast, use them for making family-pleasing Easy Vegetable Beef Soup on page 62 or the 15-minute Quick Spaghetti Supper on page 63.

Chop the beef. Place 2 cups chopped beef in each freezer or refrigerator container. Add the onions and 1/4 cup beef juices to each container. Cover and refrigerate up to 4 days or freeze up to 4 months. To thaw frozen beef mixture, place container in the refrigerator about 8 hours.

1. Trim excess fat from beef. Heat oil in 10-inch skillet over medium-high heat. Cook beef in oil about 10 minutes, turning occasionally, until brown on all sides. Sprinkle with salt and pepper.

2. Place onions in 3 1/2- to 6-quart slow cooker. Place beef on onions.

3. Mix remaining ingredients; pour over beef and onions. Cover and cook on low heat setting 8 to 10 hours or until beef is tender.

4. Remove beef and onions from cooker, using slotted spoon. Cut beef into slices. Skim fat from beef juices in cooker if desired. Serve beef with juices.

1 Serving: Calories 205 (Calories from Fat 100); Fat 11g (Saturated 4g); Cholesterol 55mg; Sodium 420mg; Carbohydrate 8g (Dietary Fiber 1g); Protein 20g

% Daily Value: Vitamin A 0%; Vitamin C 2%; Calcium 2%; Iron 12%

Diet Exchanges: 2 Medium-Fat Meat, 2 Vegetable

what a
Great Idea...

Caramelized Onion Pot Roast ➤

...for Leftovers

What a Great Idea ... for Leftovers!

Supper will be on the table in just 20 minutes starting with a container of leftover Caramelized Onion Pot Roast (page 60). These two heartwarming recipes are short on time, but, oh so long on flavor.

Easy Vegetable-Beef Soup

PREP TIME: 5 minutes • COOK TIME: 15 minutes

■ *4 servings* ■

1 container (2 cups) Caramelized Onion Pot Roast (page 60), thawed if frozen

2 cups frozen mixed vegetables

1/4 cup uncooked quick-cooking barley

3 cups beef broth

1 teaspoon Dijon mustard

1. Mix all ingredients in 3-quart saucepan. Heat to boiling; reduce heat to low.

2. Cover and simmer about 12 minutes or until barley is tender.

1 Serving: Calories 300 (Calories from Fat 160); Fat 18g (Saturated 7g); Cholesterol 50mg; Sodium 900mg; Carbohydrate 18g (Dietary Fiber 4g); Protein 20g

% Daily Value: Vitamin A 16%; Vitamin C 14%; Calcium 4%; Iron 14%

Diet Exchanges: 1 Starch, 2 Medium-Fat Meat, 1 Vegetable, 1 Fat

Quick Spaghetti Supper

PREP TIME: 5 minutes • COOK TIME: 10 minutes

■ *4 servings* ■

1 container (2 cups) Caramelized
Onion Pot Roast (page 60),
thawed if frozen

1 jar (16 ounces) spaghetti sauce
(any flavor)

6 cups hot cooked spaghetti, for
serving

Grated Parmesan cheese, if desired

1. Heat roast mixture and spaghetti sauce in 3-quart saucepan over medium heat about 10 minutes, stirring occasionally, until hot.

2. Serve sauce over spaghetti. Sprinkle with cheese.

1 Serving: Calories 645 (Calories from Fat 210); Fat 23g (Saturated 7g); Cholesterol 50mg; Sodium 850mg; Carbohydrate 87g (Dietary Fiber 5g); Protein 27g

% Daily Value: Vitamin A 8%; Vitamin C 16%; Calcium 30%; Iron 0%

Diet Exchanges: 5 Starch, 1 High-Fat Meat, 2 Vegetable, 2 Fat

Brisket with Cranberry Gravy

■ 8 servings ■

SLOW COOKER:
4- to 6-quart

PREP TIME:
10 minutes

COOK TIME:
Low 8 to 10 hours

Betty's Success Tip

Be sure to use a fresh beef brisket instead of a corned beef brisket. A "corned" brisket is a fresh brisket that has been cured in seasoned brine, which would overpower the delicate flavor of the cranberry gravy. If a fresh brisket isn't available, use the same cut of beef roast that you use for your favorite pot roast.

Ingredient Substitution

We like the appearance of the whole berry cranberry sauce, but you can use a can of jellied cranberries if you like. Cranberries are native to North America. Pilgrims noticed that cranes flew in great flocks to the cranberry bogs and feasted on the sour red berries. Thus the berries got the name "craneberries," which later became "cranberries."

2 1/2-pound fresh beef brisket (not corned beef)

1/2 teaspoon salt

1/4 teaspoon pepper

1 can (16 ounces) whole berry cranberry sauce

1 can (8 ounces) tomato sauce

1 medium onion, chopped (1/2 cup)

1 tablespoon mustard

1. Trim excess fat from beef. Rub surface of beef with salt and pepper. Place beef in 4- to 6-quart slow cooker. Mix remaining ingredients; pour over beef.

2. Cover and cook on low heat setting 8 to 10 hours or until beef is tender.

3. Cut beef across grain into thin slices. Skim fat from cranberry sauce in cooker if desired; serve with beef.

1 Serving: Calories 265 (Calories from Fat 70); Fat 8g (Saturated 3g); Cholesterol 60mg; Sodium 410mg; Carbohydrate 25g (Dietary Fiber 1g); Protein 24g

% Daily Value: Vitamin A 2%; Vitamin C 4%; Calcium 2%; Iron 12%

Diet Exchanges: 1 Starch, 2 1/2 Lean Meat, 2 Vegetable

Mexicali Round Steak

6 servings

SLOW COOKER:
3 1/2- to 6-quart

PREP TIME:
15 minutes

COOK TIME:
Low 8 to 9 hours

Betty's Success Tip

Not everyone loves the assertive flavor of cilantro. When you cook cilantro for a long time, however, the flavor becomes very mild and blends into the overall flavor of the dish. When it is added at the end of cooking or used fresh, it can be the primary flavor. So give this recipe a try, and see whether the one who doesn't love cilantro even knows it's in the dish.

Ingredient Substitution

Vary the taste of this all-in-one meal by using pinto beans instead of the black beans and sprinkling with Cheddar cheese in place of the Monterey Jack cheese.

Finishing Touch

Serve with additional salsa to spoon on top of each serving, and sprinkle with additional chopped fresh cilantro. Pass a basket of warm tortillas to enjoy with this hearty steak meal.

1 1/2 pounds beef boneless round steak

1 cup frozen whole kernel corn, thawed

1 cup chopped fresh cilantro

1/2 cup beef broth

3 medium stalks celery, thinly sliced (1 1/2 cups)

1 large onion, sliced

1 jar (20 ounces) salsa

1 can (15 ounces) black beans, rinsed and drained

1 cup shredded Monterey Jack cheese with jalapeño peppers (4 ounces)

1. Trim excess fat from beef. Cut beef into 6 serving pieces. Place beef in 3 1/2- to 6-quart slow cooker. Mix remaining ingredients except cheese; pour over beef.

2. Cover and cook on low heat setting 8 to 9 hours or until beef is tender.

3. Sprinkle cheese over beef mixture.

1 Serving: Calories 320 (Calories from Fat 90); Fat 10g (Saturated 5g); Cholesterol 75mg; Sodium 760mg; Carbohydrate 32g (Dietary Fiber 8g); Protein 34g

% Daily Value: Vitamin A 14%; Vitamin C 20%; Calcium 24%; Iron 26%

Diet Exchanges: 1 Starch, 3 Lean Meat, 3 Vegetable

Swiss Steak Supper

■ *6 servings* ■

SLOW COOKER:
3 1/2- to 6-quart

PREP TIME:
15 minutes

COOK TIME:
Low 7 to 9 hours

1 1/2 pounds beef boneless round steak

1/2 teaspoon peppered seasoned salt

6 to 8 new potatoes, cut into fourths

1 1/2 cups baby-cut carrots

1 medium onion, sliced

1 can (14 1/2 ounces) diced tomatoes with basil, garlic and oregano, undrained

1 jar (12 ounces) home-style beef gravy

Chopped fresh parsley, if desired

1. Trim excess fat from beef. Cut beef into 6 serving pieces. Spray 12-inch skillet with cooking spray; heat over medium-high heat. Sprinkle beef with seasoned salt. Cook beef in skillet about 8 minutes, turning once, until brown.

2. Layer potatoes, carrots, beef and onion in 3 1/2- to 6-quart slow cooker. Mix tomatoes and gravy; spoon over beef and vegetables.

3. Cover and cook on low heat setting 7 to 9 hours or until beef and vegetables are tender. Sprinkle with parsley.

Betty's Success Tip

New potatoes are thin-skinned, small, young potatoes of any variety. They are waxy in texture because there hasn't been enough time for the sugar to convert to starch. Leaving the peel on the potatoes not only retains nutrients but also helps them to keep their shape during cooking.

Ingredient Substitution

Out of tomatoes with basil, garlic and oregano? Use a can of diced tomatoes, and add 1/2 teaspoon dried basil leaves, 1/4 teaspoon garlic powder and 1/2 teaspoon dried oregano leaves. And if you have only seasoned salt, use the same amount as the peppered seasoned salt and add 1/4 teaspoon black pepper.

Serving Suggestion

Eating enough servings of vegetables in one day is not always easy. This one-dish meal already has potatoes and carrots. Serve a green vegetable not only to add more color to your plate but also to provide half of your servings of vegetables for the day.

1 Serving: Calories 230 (Calories from Fat 45); Fat 5g (Saturated 2g); Cholesterol 55mg; Sodium 590mg; Carbohydrate 24g (Dietary Fiber 3g); Protein 25g

% Daily Value: Vitamin A 50%; Vitamin C 16%; Calcium 4%; Iron 20%

Diet Exchanges: 1 Starch, 2 1/2 Very Lean Meat, 2 Vegetable

Hungarian Goulash

8 servings

SLOW COOKER:
3 1/2- to 6-quart

PREP TIME:
20 minutes

COOK TIME:
Low 8 to 10 hours
High 4 to 5 hours

FINISHING COOK TIME:
High 30 minutes

Ingredient Substitution

Just discovered you are all out of fresh garlic? Use 1/4 teaspoon garlic powder instead.

Finishing Touch

For a special touch, top each serving of goulash with a dollop of sour cream or toss the hot noodles with a tablespoon or two of poppy seed.

2 tablespoons vegetable oil

2 pounds beef stew meat, cut into 1-inch pieces

1 large onion, sliced

1 can (14 1/2 ounces) ready-to-serve beef broth

1 can (6 ounces) tomato paste

2 cloves garlic, finely chopped

1 tablespoon Worcestershire sauce

1 tablespoon paprika

1 teaspoon salt

1/4 teaspoon caraway seed, if desired

1/4 teaspoon pepper

1/4 cup cold water

3 tablespoons all-purpose flour

1 medium bell pepper, cut into strips

8 cups hot cooked noodles, for serving

1. Heat oil in 10-inch skillet over medium-high heat. Cook beef in oil about 10 minutes, stirring occasionally, until brown; drain. Place beef and onion in 3 1/2- to 6-quart slow cooker.

2. Mix broth, tomato paste, garlic, Worcestershire sauce, paprika, salt, caraway seed and pepper; stir into beef mixture.

3. Cover and cook on low heat setting 8 to 10 hours until beef is tender.

4. Mix water and flour; gradually stir into beef mixture. Stir in bell pepper. Cover and cook on high heat setting 30 minutes.

5. Serve goulash over noodles.

1 Serving: Calories 435 (Calories from Fat 135); Fat 15g (Saturated 5g); Cholesterol 110mg; Sodium 770mg; Carbohydrate 50g (Dietary Fiber 4g); Protein 29g

% Daily Value: Vitamin A 12%; Vitamin C 20%; Calcium 4%; Iron 32%

Diet Exchanges: 3 Starch, 2 1/2 Medium-Fat Meat, 1 Vegetable

Hungarian Goulash ➤

Beef Stroganoff

■ 8 servings ■

SLOW COOKER:
3 1/2- to 6-quart

PREP TIME:
10 minutes

COOK TIME:
Low 8 to 10 hours

Betty's Success Tip

The soups not only add flavor but also provide a nice smooth creamy sauce for this stroganoff. The sour cream is stirred in at the end of cooking so it stays smooth and doesn't curdle the sauce.

Finishing Touch

Make this stroganoff extra special by replacing the canned mushrooms with sliced fresh mushrooms you add at the end of cooking. Sauté the mushrooms in a small amount of butter just until they brown. Stir mushrooms, and any remaining butter, in with the sour cream. Top off the stroganoff with a generous sprinkle of freshly chopped parsley.

2 pounds beef stew meat

1 large onion, chopped (1 cup)

1 can (10 3/4 ounces) condensed cream of golden mushroom soup

1 can (10 3/4 ounces) condensed cream of onion soup

1 can (8 ounces) sliced mushrooms, drained

1/4 teaspoon pepper

1 package (8 ounces) cream cheese, cubed

1 container (8 ounces) sour cream

6 cups hot cooked noodles or rice, for serving, if desired

1. Mix beef, onion, soups, mushrooms and pepper in 3 1/2- to 6-quart slow cooker.

2. Cover and cook on low heat setting 8 to 10 hours or until beef is very tender.

3. Stir cream cheese into beef mixture until melted. Stir in sour cream.

4. Serve beef mixture over noodles.

1 Serving: Calories 505 (Calories from Fat 325); Fat 36g (Saturated 17g); Cholesterol 145mg; Sodium 830mg; Carbohydrate 12g (Dietary Fiber 1g); Protein 34g

% Daily Value: Vitamin A 14%; Vitamin C 2%; Calcium 12%; Iron 22%

Diet Exchanges: 4 High-Fat Meat, 2 Vegetable, 1 Fat

Spinach-Stuffed Cubed Steaks

■ *4 servings* ■

SLOW COOKER:
2- to 3 1/2-quart

PREP TIME:
20 minutes

COOK TIME:
Low 8 to 9 hours

FINISHING COOK TIME:
10 minutes

Betty's Success Tip

Flatten the cubed steaks by placing them between sheets of plastic wrap or waxed paper and pounding with the flat side of a meat mallet or a rolling pin. Don't have a meat mallet or rolling pin? Press the heel of your hand over the top of the steak until it is evenly flattened.

Ingredient Substitution

Traditional pesto is a mixture of basil, garlic, olive oil and pine nuts. Today, however, this popular sauce can be made from other herbs and vegetables instead of basil. There is sun-dried tomato, roasted bell pepper and spinach pesto, just to mention a few, so use whichever pesto you like.

Finishing Touch

To add crunch and bright red color to this dish, add a chopped small red bell pepper to the sauce when you stir in the cornstarch mixture.

4 beef cubed steaks (about 1 1/4 pounds)

1/4 cup basil pesto

1 tablespoon plus 1 teaspoon instant minced onion

1 package (10 ounces) frozen chopped spinach, thawed and squeezed to drain

1/2 cup beef broth

1 teaspoon finely chopped garlic

1 tablespoon cornstarch

1 tablespoon water

1. Flatten each beef steak to 1/8-inch thickness. Spread 1 tablespoon pesto over each steak; sprinkle each with 1 teaspoon onion. Divide spinach among steaks, spreading to edges. Roll up steaks; secure with toothpicks.

2. Place steaks in 2- to 3 1/2-quart slow cooker. Mix broth and garlic; pour over steaks.

3. Cover and cook on low heat setting 8 to 9 hours or until beef is tender.

4. Remove steaks from cooker to serving platter; keep warm.

5. Skim fat from beef juices in cooker if desired. Measure 1 cup juices; pour into small saucepan. Mix cornstarch and water; stir into juices. Cook over medium-high heat about 5 minutes, stirring frequently, until thickened. Serve over steaks.

1 Serving: Calories 250 (Calories from Fat 110); Fat 12g (Saturated 3g); Cholesterol 75mg; Sodium 300mg; Carbohydrate 7g (Dietary Fiber 2g); Protein 31g

% Daily Value: Vitamin A 36%; Vitamin C 6%; Calcium 12%; Iron 20%

Diet Exchanges: 4 Lean Meat, 1 Vegetable

Picadillo

■ *12 servings* ■

SLOW COOKER:
3 1/2- to 6-quart

PREP TIME:
20 minutes

COOK TIME:
Low 3 to 4 hours

What a Great Idea. . .
for Leftovers

This Mexican version of hash is great to have as a standby in the freezer. It adds a unique flavor twist to Picadillo Tacos (page 74) and Hash 'n Eggs (page 75). And use it as a filling the next time you make enchiladadas or tostadas.

Place 2 cups Picadillo in each freezer or refrigerator container. Cover and refrigerate up to 4 days or freeze up to 4 months. To thaw frozen Picadillo, place container in the refrigerator about 8 hours.

2 pounds ground beef

1 large onion, chopped (1 cup)

1 cup raisins

2 teaspoons chili powder

1 teaspoon salt

3/4 teaspoon ground cinnamon

1/2 teaspoon ground cumin

1/2 teaspoon pepper

2 cloves garlic, finely chopped

2 medium apples, peeled and chopped

2 cans (10 ounces each) diced tomatoes and green chilies, undrained

1/2 cup slivered almonds, toasted (page 152)

1. Cook beef and onion in 12-inch skillet over medium heat, stirring occasionally, until beef is brown; drain.

2. Mix beef mixture and remaining ingredients except almonds in 3 1/2- to 6-quart slow cooker.

3. Cover and cook on low heat setting 3 to 4 hours or until most of the liquid is absorbed. Stir in almonds.

1 Serving: Calories 245 (Calories from Fat 115); Fat 13g (Saturated 5g); Cholesterol 45mg; Sodium 310mg; Carbohydrate 18g (Dietary Fiber 2g); Protein 16g

% Daily Value: Vitamin A 4%; Vitamin C 8%; Calcium 4%; Iron 12%

Diet Exchanges: 2 Medium-Fat Meat, 1 Vegetable, 1 Fruit

what a
Great Idea...

Picadillo ➤

Betty Crocker®

Off Low High

...for Leftovers ➤

What a Great Idea ... for Leftovers!

Picadillo (page 72) is made with a combination of ingredients that might surprise you—ground beef, apples, raisins, and almonds. The flavors and textures add a distinctive flair to these recipes.

Picadillo Tacos

PREP TIME: 5 minutes • COOK TIME: 5 minutes

■ *4 servings* ■

1 container (2 cups) Picadillo (page 72), thawed if frozen

8 taco shells

2 cups shredded lettuce

1 medium tomato, chopped (3/4 cup)

1 cup shredded Monterey Jack cheese (4 ounces)

1 cup sour cream

1. Heat Picadillo in small saucepan over medium heat about 5 minutes, stirring occasionally, until hot.

2. Fill taco shells with Picadillo. Top with remaining ingredients.

1 Serving: Calories 540 (Calories from Fat 325); Fat 36g (Saturated 17g); Cholesterol 95mg; Sodium 580mg; Carbohydrate 35g (Dietary Fiber 4g); Protein 23g

% Daily Value: Vitamin A 22%; Vitamin C 10%; Calcium 14%; Iron 34%

Diet Exchanges: 2 Starch, 2 Medium-Fat Meat, 1 Vegetable

Hash 'n Eggs

PREP TIME: 5 minutes • COOK TIME: 10 minutes

■ *4 servings* ■

1 container (2 cups) Picadillo
  (page 72), thawed if frozen

1 tablespoon margarine or butter

4 eggs

1/4 teaspoon salt

1/2 cup salsa

1/4 cup shredded Cheddar cheese
  (1 ounce)

1. Heat Picadillo in small saucepan over medium heat about 5 minutes, stirring occasionally, until hot.

2. Meanwhile, heat margarine in 10-inch skillet over medium heat. Crack eggs and slide each into skillet; reduce heat to low. Cook 3 minutes; sprinkle with salt. Turn eggs over; cook 1 to 2 minutes longer or until eggs are set.

3. Divide Picadillo among 4 plates. Top each with fried egg. Top with salsa; sprinkle with cheese.

1 Serving: Calories 330 (Calories from Fat 190); Fat 21g (Saturated 7g); Cholesterol 250mg; Sodium 650mg; Carbohydrate 17g (Dietary Fiber 2g); Protein 20g

% Daily Value: Vitamin A 16%; Vitamin C 10%; Calcium 10%; Iron 12%

Diet Exchanges: 1 Starch, 2 Medium-Fat Meat, 2 Fat

Cabbage Roll Casserole

■ *6 servings* ■

SLOW COOKER:
3 1/2- to 6-quart

PREP TIME:
15 minutes

COOK TIME:
Low 4 to 6 hours

Betty's Success Tip

It is important to cook the ground beef before adding it to the cooker. Because the beef is ground, there is a greater risk that bacteria may start to grow before the temperature inside the cooker gets high enough.

Ingredient Substitution

No coleslaw mix on hand? Substitute 4 1/2 cups shredded cabbage and one shredded carrot. If you own a food processor with a shredding attachment, this is a great time to use it.

Finishing Touch

Place squares of process American cheese over the top of the finished casserole, or sprinkle with shredded Cheddar cheese. Cover and let it stand a few minutes so the cheese melts. Kids will love it!

1 pound ground beef

1 medium onion, chopped (1/2 cup)

5 cups coleslaw mix

1/2 cup uncooked instant rice

1/4 cup water

2 teaspoons paprika

1/2 teaspoon salt

1/4 teaspoon pepper

1 can (15 ounces) chunky Italian-style tomato sauce

1. Cook beef and onion in 10-inch skillet over medium heat, stirring occasionally, until beef is brown; drain.

2. Mix beef mixture and remaining ingredients in 3 1/2- to 6-quart slow cooker. (Cooker will be very full, but cabbage will cook down.)

3. Cover and cook on low heat setting 4 to 6 hours or until cabbage is tender.

1 Serving: Calories 300 (Calories from Fat 125); Fat 14g (Saturated 5g); Cholesterol 45mg; Sodium 600mg; Carbohydrate 27g (Dietary Fiber 3g); Protein 17g

% Daily Value: Vitamin A 24%; Vitamin C 28%; Calcium 6%; Iron 14%

Diet Exchanges: 1 Starch, 1 1/2 High-Fat Meat, 2 Vegetable

Veal Paprika

■ *6 servings* ■

SLOW COOKER:
3 1/2- to 6-quart

PREP TIME:
20 minutes

COOK TIME:
Low 6 to 8 hours

Betty's Success Tip

Paprika not only adds flavor to dishes but also adds color and a delightful aroma. The flavor of paprika can range from mild to pungent and hot, and the color can vary from orange-red to a very deep red. Most supermarkets carry only mild paprika, so you may want to check at an ethnic market for a more flavorful, hotter Hungarian paprika.

Ingredient Substitution

The flavor of paprika is also excellent with beef, so try this savory dish with beef stew meat.

Finishing Touch

Toss the noodles with poppy seed for a little crunch before serving with the veal mixture. To complement the flavor of the paprika, spoon a dollop of sour cream on top of each serving. A sprinkle of chopped fresh dill weed also adds a "fresh-flavor" lift to this dish.

3 tablespoons all-purpose flour

3/4 teaspoon salt

1 1/2 pounds veal stew meat

2 tablespoons vegetable oil

1 medium onion, chopped (1/2 cup)

1 can (8 ounces) tomato sauce

1 can (5 ounces) evaporated milk

2 tablespoons paprika

1 tablespoon Worcestershire sauce

6 cups hot cooked noodles, for serving

1. Mix flour and salt in resealable plastic bag. Add veal; shake until evenly coated. Heat oil in 10-inch skillet over medium heat. Cook veal in oil about 10 minutes, turning occasionally, until brown.

2. Mix veal and remaining ingredients except noodles in 3 1/2- to 6-quart slow cooker.

3. Cover and cook on low heat setting 6 to 8 hours or until veal is tender; stir.

4. Serve veal mixture over noodles.

1 Serving: Calories 395 (Calories from Fat 90); Fat 10g (Saturated 3g); Cholesterol 130mg; Sodium 650mg; Carbohydrate 51g (Dietary Fiber 3g); Protein 28g

% Daily Value: Vitamin A 20%; Vitamin C 6%; Calcium 12%; Iron 24%

Diet Exchanges: 3 Starch, 2 1/2 Lean Meat, 1 Vegetable

Braised Veal Shanks, Milan Style

■ *6 servings* ■

SLOW COOKER:
5- to 6-quart

PREP TIME:
30 minutes

COOK TIME:
Low 8 to 10 hours

4 pounds veal shanks

1/4 cup all-purpose flour

3 tablespoons olive or vegetable oil

1 medium onion, chopped (1/2 cup)

1 medium carrot, chopped (1/2 cup)

1 medium stalk celery, chopped (1/2 cup)

1 clove garlic, finely chopped

1/2 cup water

1/3 cup dry white wine

1 teaspoon salt

1/2 teaspoon dried basil leaves

1/2 teaspoon dried thyme leaves

1/4 teaspoon pepper

Betty's Success Tip

Veal shanks are not always available, so check with your butcher to place an order ahead if necessary. You'll also find this succulent Milan masterpiece on restaurant menus under the name *ossobuco* or *ossibuchi*, which means "a hollowed bone."

Ingredient Substitution

If your family prefers beef to veal, go ahead and use beef shank cross cuts. Check with your butcher if you don't see them in the meat case.

Finishing Touch

This dish is often served with a refreshing condiment called *gremolata*. It is easy to make. Just mix 2 tablespoons chopped fresh parsley, a finely chopped clove of garlic and 1 teaspoon grated lemon peel. Pass the gremolata at the table to sprinkle on each serving.

1. Trim excess fat from veal shanks. Coat veal with flour. Heat oil in 10-inch skillet over medium heat. Cook veal in oil about 20 minutes, turning occasionally, until brown on all sides; drain.

2. Place veal in 5- to 6-quart slow cooker. Mix remaining ingredients; pour over veal.

3. Cover and cook on low heat setting 8 to 10 hours or until veal is very tender and pulls away from bones.

4. Remove veal and vegetables from cooker, using slotted spoon; place on serving platter. Skim fat from veal juices in cooker if desired. Pour juices over veal and vegetables.

1 Serving: Calories 450 (Calories from Fat 180); Fat 20g (Saturated 6g); Cholesterol 255mg; Sodium 620mg; Carbohydrate 7g (Dietary Fiber 1g); Protein 62g

% Daily Value: Vitamin A 16%; Vitamin C 2%; Calcium 8%; Iron 18%

Diet Exchanges: 8 Lean Meat, 1 Vegetable

Pork Roast with Sherry-Plum Sauce

■ *12 servings* ■

Crowd SIZE

SLOW COOKER:
3 1/2- to 6-quart

PREP TIME:
20 minutes

COOK TIME:
Low 7 to 9 hours

FINISHING COOK TIME:
High 15 minutes

What a Great Idea. . . for Leftovers

Too much roast for one meal? The leftover meal and sauce make handy "freezer buddies" for an easy Pork and Vegetable Stir-Fry (page 82) or Warm Cabbage, Apple and Pork Salad (page 83).

Cut pork into thin strips. Place 2 cups pork in each freezer or refrigerator container. Pour 1/4 cup sauce into each container. Cover and refrigerate up to 4 days or freeze up to 4 months. To thaw frozen pork mixture, place container in the refrigerator about 8 hours.

4-pound pork boneless loin roast

2 tablespoons vegetable oil

1 cup dry sherry

1 tablespoon ground mustard (dry)

2 tablespoons soy sauce

1 1/2 teaspoons dried thyme leaves

1 1/4 teaspoons ground ginger

1 teaspoon salt

1/4 teaspoon pepper

3 cloves garlic, finely chopped

1/2 cup plum jam

1. Trim excess fat from pork. Heat oil in 10-inch skillet over medium-high heat. Cook pork in oil about 10 minutes, turning occasionally, until brown on all sides.

2. Place pork in 3 1/2- to 6-quart slow cooker. Mix remaining ingredients except jam; pour over pork.

3. Cover and cook on low heat setting 7 to 9 hours or until pork is tender.

4. Remove pork from cooker; cover and keep warm. Skim fat from pork juices in cooker if desired. Stir jam into juices.

5. Cover and cook on high heat setting about 15 minutes or until jam is melted; stir. Serve sauce with pork.

1 Serving: Calories 240 (Calories from Fat 90); Fat 10g (Saturated 3g); Cholesterol 70mg; Sodium 400mg; Carbohydrate 12g (Dietary Fiber 0g); Protein 25g

% Daily Value: Vitamin A 0%; Vitamin C 0%; Calcium 0%; Iron 6%

Diet Exchanges: 1 Starch, 3 Lean Meat

what a Great Idea...

Pork Roast with Sherry-Plum Sauce ➤

for Leftovers ▶

What a Great Idea ... for Leftovers!

Pork Roast with Sherry-Plum Sauce (page 80) makes a great "keep on hand" leftover ready to add to your favorite Asian recipe. Below are two recipes using cooked pork that we found both quick and tasty.

Pork and Vegetable Stir-Fry

PREP TIME: 10 minutes • COOK TIME: 10 minutes

■ *4 servings* ■

1/4 cup apple juice

2 tablespoons dry sherry or apple juice

2 tablespoons soy sauce

1 tablespoon cornstarch

1 tablespoon vegetable oil

1/4 cup slivered almonds

1 package (16 ounces) fresh (refrigerated) stir-fry vegetables

1 clove garlic, finely chopped

1 container (2 cups) Pork Roast with Sherry-Plum Sauce (page 80), thawed if frozen

2 cups hot cooked rice, for serving

1. Shake apple juice or sherry, soy sauce and cornstarch in tightly covered container; set aside.

2. Heat oil in 12-inch skillet or wok over medium-high heat. Add almonds; stir-fry until golden brown. Remove almonds with slotted spoon; set aside.

3. Add stir-fry vegetables and garlic to skillet; cook about 5 minutes or until vegetables are crisp-tender.

4. Add pork mixture and juice mixture to skillet. Cook 2 to 3 minutes, stirring frequently, until sauce is thickened and bubbly.

5. Serve pork mixture over rice. Sprinkle with almonds.

1 Serving: Calories 305 (Calories from Fat 145); Fat 16g (Saturated 3g); Cholesterol 50mg; Sodium 930mg; Carbohydrate 22g (Dietary Fiber 5g); Protein 23g

% Daily Value: Vitamin A 36%; Vitamin C 32%; Calcium 6%; Iron 10%

Diet Exchanges: 1 Starch, 2 Medium-Fat Meat, 1 Vegetable, 1 Fat

Warm Cabbage, Apple and Pork Salad

PREP TIME: 20 minutes • COOK TIME: 10 minutes

■ *4 servings* ■

1 container (2 cups) Pork Roast
  with Sherry-Plum Sauce (page 80),
  thawed if frozen

Plum Dressing (below)

2 teaspoons vegetable oil

2 medium apples, cut into thin
  wedges

1 small onion, sliced

6 cups coleslaw mix or shredded
  cabbage

1/2 teaspoon salt

1/4 cup plum sauce reserved from
  pork

2 tablespoons plum jam

1 tablespoon cider vinegar

2 teaspoons Dijon mustard

1/4 teaspoon pepper

1. Drain plum sauce from pork mixture; reserve for Plum Dressing. Prepare Plum Dressing; set aside.

2. Heat oil in 12-skillet over medium heat. Cover and cook apples and onion in oil 5 minutes or until onion is tender. Stir in coleslaw mix; sprinkle with salt. Cover and cook about 2 minutes or until coleslaw is crisp-tender. Remove cabbage mixture from skillet; cover and keep warm.

3. Increase heat to medium-high. Cook pork in skillet about 2 minutes, stirring frequently, until warm. Stir in dressing. Cook about 1 minute or until slightly thickened.

4. Spoon pork mixture over cabbage mixture. Serve immediately.

Plum Dressing

Shake all ingredients in tightly covered container.

1 Serving: Calories 315 (Calories from Fat 90); Fat 90g (Saturated 3g); Cholesterol 50mg; Sodium 530mg; Carbohydrate 22g (Dietary Fiber 6g); Protein 21g

% Daily Value: Vitamin A 2%; Vitamin C 42%; Calcium 8%; Iron 10%

Diet Exchanges: 1 Starch, 2 Lean Meat, 2 Vegetable, 1 Fruit, 1/2 Fat

Garlic Pork Roast

■ *10 servings* ■

Crowd
S I Z E

SLOW COOKER:
3 1/2- to 6-quart

PREP TIME:
20 minutes

COOK TIME:
Low 8 to 10 hours

What a Great Idea. . .
for Leftovers

You'll want to make this roast to shred and pop in the freezer to have for those busy days. No one will know it took you less than 30 minutes to make Weeknight Pork Stew (page 86) or Spicy Pork Chili (page 87).

Remove pork from the cooking liquid; reserve the liquid. Cool pork slightly. Shred warm pork, using 2 forks. Place 2 cups shredded pork in each refrigerator or freezer container. Add 1/4 cup reserved cooking liquid to each container. Cover and refrigerate up to 4 days or freeze up to 4 months. To thaw frozen pork mixture, place container in the refrigerator about 8 hours.

3 1/2-pound pork boneless loin roast

1 tablespoon vegetable oil

1 teaspoon salt

1/2 teaspoon pepper

1 medium onion, sliced

3 cloves garlic, peeled

1 cup chicken broth or water

1. Trim excess fat from pork. Heat oil in 10-inch skillet over medium-high heat. Cook pork in oil about 10 minutes, turning occasionally, until brown on all sides. Sprinkle with salt and pepper.

2. Place onion and garlic in 3 1/2- to 6-quart slow cooker. Place pork on onion and garlic. Pour broth over pork.

3. Cover and cook on low heat setting 8 to 10 hours or until pork is tender.

1 Serving: Calories 200 (Calories from Fat 90); Fat 10g (Saturated 3g); Cholesterol 75mg; Sodium 280mg; Carbohydrate 2g (Dietary Fiber 0g); Protein 26g

% Daily Value: Vitamin A 0%; Vitamin C 0%; Calcium 0%; Iron 4%

Diet Exchanges: 4 Lean Meat

what a
Great Idea...

Garlic Pork Roast ➤

...for Leftovers

Your family will quickly gather around the table when you serve these hearty dishes using leftover Garlic Pork Roast (page 84). No one can resist the subtle aroma of garlic when it fills the air!

Weeknight Pork Stew

PREP TIME: 10 minutes • COOK TIME: 20 minutes

■ *4 servings* ■

1 container (2 cups) Garlic Pork Roast (page 84), thawed if frozen

8 small new potatoes, cut into 1/4-inch slices

2/3 cup vegetable, chicken or beef broth

1 1/4 teaspoons dried basil leaves

1/2 teaspoon salt

1 cup frozen green peas

2 teaspoons cornstarch

2 teaspoons water

1. Mix all ingredients except peas, cornstarch and water in 3-quart saucepan. Heat to boiling; reduce heat to low. Cover and simmer 10 to 12 minutes or until potatoes are tender.

2. Rinse peas with cold water to separate; stir into pork mixture. Cover and cook 2 minutes.

3. Mix cornstarch and water; stir into pork mixture. Cook and stir about 1 minute or until sauce is thickened.

1 Serving: Calories 220 (Calories from Fat 55); Fat 6g (Saturated 2g); Cholesterol 45mg; Sodium 670mg; Carbohydrate 27g (Dietary Fiber 4g); Protein 19g

% Daily Value: Vitamin A 4%; Vitamin C 12%; Calcium 2%; Iron 12%

Diet Exchanges: 1 Starch, 2 Lean Meat, 2 Vegetable

Spicy Pork Chili

PREP TIME: 5 minutes • COOK TIME: 15 minutes

■ *4 servings* ■

1 container (2 cups) Garlic Pork Roast (page 84), thawed if frozen

1 cup hot or medium salsa

1 to 2 teaspoons chili powder

1 can (15 or 16 ounces) pinto or kidney beans, rinsed and drained

1/2 cup shredded Colby-Monterey Jack cheese (2 ounces)

4 medium green onions, sliced (1/4 cup)

Sour cream, if desired

1. Mix all ingredients except cheese, onions and sour cream in 3-quart saucepan. Heat to boiling; reduce heat to low. Cover and simmer about 10 minutes or until hot.

2. Sprinkle each serving with cheese and onions. Top with sour cream.

1 Serving: Calories 300 (Calories from Fat 100); Fat 11g (Saturated 5g); Cholesterol 60mg; Sodium 610mg; Carbohydrate 32g (Dietary Fiber 11g); Protein 29g

% Daily Value: Vitamin A 10%; Vitamin C 14%; Calcium 16%; Iron 22%

Diet Exchanges: 2 Starch, 3 Lean Meat

Pork Roast with Creamy Mustard Sauce

8 servings

SLOW COOKER:
3 1/2- to 6-quart

PREP TIME:
15 minutes

COOK TIME:
Low 7 to 9 hours

FINISHING COOK TIME:
High 15 minutes

Betty's Success Tip

To make quick work of chopping the vegetables, place them in a food processor and chop until fine.

Ingredient Substitution

White wine blends nicely with the flavor of mustard. If you don't have wine on hand, you can use chicken broth.

Serving Suggestion

Want to serve potatoes but tired of the same old boiled or baked potato? For a change, serve potato dumplings, German spaetzle or Italian gnocchi. The kids will think they're fun to eat. You will find them in the frozen section at the supermarket. Or look for a box of gnocchi in the dried pasta section of the store. Toss the cooked dumplings with melted butter, and add a sprinkle of chopped fresh parsley or dill weed for a touch of color and flavor.

2 1/2- to 3-pound pork boneless sirloin roast

1 tablespoon vegetable oil

3/4 cup dry white wine

2 tablespoons all-purpose flour

1 teaspoon salt

1/2 teaspoon pepper

2 medium carrots, finely chopped or shredded

1 medium onion, finely chopped (1/2 cup)

1 small shallot, finely chopped (2 tablespoons)

1/4 cup half-and-half

2 to 3 tablespoons country-style Dijon mustard

1. Trim excess fat from pork. Heat oil in 10-inch skillet over medium-high heat. Cook pork in oil about 10 minutes, turning occasionally, until brown on all sides.

2. Place pork in 3 1/2- to 6-quart slow cooker. Mix remaining ingredients except half-and-half and mustard; pour over pork.

3. Cover and cook on low heat setting 7 to 9 hours or until pork is tender.

4. Remove pork from cooker; cover and keep warm. Skim fat from pork juices in cooker if desired. Stir half-and-half and mustard into juices.

5. Cover and cook on high heat setting about 15 minutes or until slightly thickened. Serve sauce with pork.

1 Serving: Calories 175 (Calories from Fat 80); Fat 9g (Saturated 3g); Cholesterol 55mg; Sodium 390mg; Carbohydrate 5g (Dietary Fiber 1g); Protein 20g

% Daily Value: Vitamin A 24%; Vitamin C 2%; Calcium 2%; Iron 6%

Diet Exchanges: 2 1/2 Lean Meat, 1 Vegetable

Pork Chop Dinner with Apples and Squash

■ 4 servings ■

SLOW COOKER:
3 1/2- to 6-quart

PREP TIME:
20 minutes

COOK TIME:
Low 8 to 9 hours

1 small butternut squash

3 large unpeeled cooking apples

4 pork loin chops, 3/4 inch thick (about 1 1/4 pounds)

3/4 cup sugar

2 tablespoons all-purpose flour

1 teaspoon ground cinnamon

1/2 teaspoon salt

1. Peel squash. Cut squash in half; remove seeds. Cut squash into 1/2-inch slices. Cut apples into fourths; remove cores. Cut apple pieces crosswise in half. Remove excess fat from pork.

2. Layer squash and apples in 3 1/2- to 6-quart slow cooker. Mix remaining ingredients. Coat pork with sugar mixture. Place pork on apples. Sprinkle with any remaining sugar mixture.

3. Cover and cook on low heat setting 8 to 9 hours or until pork is tender.

1 Serving: Calories 440 (Calories from Fat 80); Fat 9g (Saturated 3g); Cholesterol 65mg; Sodium 340mg; Carbohydrate 71g (Dietary Fiber 5g); Protein 24g

% Daily Value: Vitamin A 38%; Vitamin C 14%; Calcium 4%; Iron 10%

Diet Exchanges: 2 Starch, 2 Lean Meat, 2 Vegetable, 2 Fruit

Betty's Success Tip

You will want to use a variety of apple that will hold its shape rather than one that will become soft during cooking. Rome Beauty is a good choice. Also, the red color of its skin holds well, and some of the color will bleed into the flesh of the apple pieces during cooking to give it a rosy color.

Ingredient Substitution

Butternut squash resembles the shape of a light bulb or pear— wider at one end than the other. It usually weighs between 2 and 3 pounds and has a golden yellow to camel-colored shell. You also can use about 2 pounds of other winter squash, such as hubbard, buttercup or banana, cut into pieces.

Finishing Touch

Add a wonderful nutty flavor and crunch by sprinkling coarsely chopped toasted nuts over each serving. Try pecans, walnuts, hazelnuts or your favorite nut.

Pork Chops with Mixed Dried Fruit

▪ *4 servings* ▪

SLOW COOKER:
3 1/2- or 6-quart

PREP TIME:
15 minutes

COOK TIME:
Low 6 to 7 hours

FINISHING COOK TIME:
High 6 minutes

4 pork loin chops, about 3/4 inch thick (about 1 1/4 pounds)

1 package (8 ounces) mixed dried fruit (1 1/2 cups)

3 tablespoons packed brown sugar

3 tablespoons orange marmalade

2 tablespoons cider vinegar

1/2 teaspoon ground ginger

1 can (5 1/2 ounces) apricot nectar

1 tablespoon cornstarch

2 tablespoons water

1. Place pork in 3 1/2- or 6-quart slow cooker. Layer dried fruit evenly over pork. Mix brown sugar, marmalade, vinegar, ginger and nectar; pour over pork and fruit.

2. Cover and cook on low heat setting 6 to 7 hours or until pork is slightly pink when cut near bone.

3. Remove pork and fruit from cooker, using slotted spoon; cover and keep warm.

4. Skim fat from pork juices in cooker if desired. Pour juices into 1-quart saucepan. Mix cornstarch and water; stir into juices. Cook on high heat 4 to 6 minutes, stirring constantly, until thickened and bubbly. Serve sauce with pork and fruit.

Betty's Success Tip

Check that the package of dried fruit contains large pieces of fruit, such as slices of peaches, apples, pears and apricots. Diced dried fruit is also available, but the pieces are so small that they over-cook and become part of the sauce during the long, slow cooking.

Ingredient Substitution

Although apricot nectar enhances the flavors of the dried fruit, feel free to also use 3/4 cup of another light-colored fruit juice, such as apple, orange or pineapple.

Serving Suggestion

Parsley-buttered new potatoes and steamed baby carrots are all that is needed to complete this Scandinavian-influenced dish and satisfy everyone at dinner.

1 Serving: Calories 395 (Calories from Fat 70); Fat 8g (Saturated 3g); Cholesterol 65mg; Sodium 60mg; Carbohydrate 61g (Dietary Fiber 4g); Protein 24g

% Daily Value: Vitamin A 18%; Vitamin C 2%; Calcium 4%; Iron 14%

Diet Exchanges: 2 Starch, 2 1/2 Lean Meat, 2 Fruit

Pork Chops with Mixed Dried Fruit ➤

Smoky-Flavored Barbecued Ribs

■ 4 servings ■

SLOW COOKER:
5- to 6-quart

PREP TIME:
15 minutes

COOK TIME:
Low 8 to 9 hours

FINISHING COOK TIME:
Low 1 hour

Ingredient Substitution

Cola adds a wonderful sweetness to the ribs, but you can use water instead if you don't have any cola on hand. Pork ribs are by far the most popular choice for barbecued ribs, but try beef short ribs for a change. Trim any excess fat from the short ribs before adding them to the cooker.

Serving Suggestion

Busy day? Stop at the deli and pick up some potato salad and baked beans for an easy, old-fashioned southern barbecued rib dinner.

3 1/2 pounds pork loin back ribs

1/4 cup packed brown sugar

1/2 teaspoon pepper

3 tablespoons liquid smoke

2 cloves garlic, finely chopped

1 teaspoon salt

1 medium onion, sliced

1/2 cup cola

1 1/2 cups barbecue sauce

1. Spray inside of 5- to 6-quart slow cooker with cooking spray.

2. Remove inner skin from ribs. Mix brown sugar, pepper, liquid smoke, garlic and salt; rub mixture into ribs. Cut ribs into about 4-inch pieces. Layer ribs and onion in slow cooker. Pour cola over ribs.

3. Cover and cook on low heat setting 8 to 9 hours or until ribs are tender. Remove ribs from cooker. Drain liquid from cooker and discard.

4. Pour barbecue sauce into shallow bowl. Dip ribs into sauce. Place ribs in cooker. Pour any remaining sauce over ribs. Cover and cook on low heat setting 1 hour.

1 Serving: Calories 890 (Calories from Fat 540); Fat 60g (Saturated 22g); Cholesterol 230mg; Sodium 1540mg; Carbohydrate 32g (Dietary Fiber 2g); Protein 58g

% Daily Value: Vitamin A 8%; Vitamin C 6%; Calcium 12%; Iron 26%

Diet Exchanges: 2 Starch, 7 High-Fat Meat

Scalloped Potato and Sausage Supper

■ 4 servings ■

SLOW COOKER:
3 1/2- to 6-quart

PREP TIME:
10 minutes

COOK TIME:
Low 4 to 5 hours

FINISHING COOK TIME:
Low 5 minutes

Betty's Success Tip

If you are watching the sodium and fat in your diet, use reduced-fat sausage and reduced-sodium soup in this all-family favorite.

Ingredient Substitution

Check your cupboard and discover that you have other cans of cream soup but not cream of mushroom with garlic? Use one of the other cream soups, and add 1/4 teaspoon of garlic powder.

Serving Suggestion

This dish makes a great family dinner on a busy fall evening. Add a crisp green tossed salad and some long, thin, crunchy breadsticks.

1 package (5 ounces) scalloped potato mix

1 can (10 3/4 ounces) condensed cream of mushroom with garlic soup

1 soup can water

1 pound fully cooked kielbasa sausage, cut into 2-inch diagonal pieces

1 cup frozen green peas

1. Spray 3 1/2- to 6-quart slow cooker with cooking spray. Place uncooked potatoes in slow cooker. Mix soup, water and Sauce Mix (from potato mix); pour over potatoes. Top with sausage.

2. Cover and cook on low heat setting 4 to 5 hours or until potatoes are tender.

3. Rinse peas with cold water to separate. Sprinkle peas over potatoes. Cover and cook on low heat setting about 5 minutes or until peas are hot.

1 Serving: Calories 400 (Calories from Fat 305); Fat 34g (Saturated 12g); Cholesterol 65mg; Sodium 1460mg; Carbohydrate 10g (Dietary Fiber 2g); Protein 16g

% Daily Value: Vitamin A 2%; Vitamin C 2%; Calcium 4%; Iron 10%

Diet Exchanges: 2 High-Fat Meat, 2 Vegetable, 3 Fat

Lamb Dijon

■ 6 servings ■

SLOW COOKER:
3 1/2- to 6-quart

PREP TIME:
25 minutes

COOK TIME:
Low 8 to 10 hours
High 4 to 5 hours

FINISHING COOK TIME:
High 15 minutes

Betty's Success Tip

Grate the lemon peel before squeezing the lemon for juice, being careful to grate only the yellow part of the peel because the white pith is very bitter. To get the most juice from a lemon, roll it on a counter while pushing down firmly to break the tissues inside, which will release the juice. Or heat the lemon in the microwave for a minute, which also helps to release the juice.

Ingredient Substitution

For a Dijon-flavored beef dish, use the same amount of beef stew meat instead of lamb.

Finishing Touch

Gremolata, which is served with Italian braised veal shanks, would also be yummy sprinkled over this lamb dish. Just mix 2 tablespoons chopped fresh parsley, a finely chopped clove of garlic and 1 teaspoon grated lemon peel. Sprinkle it over each serving of lamb.

1/4 cup all-purpose flour

1 teaspoon salt

1/4 teaspoon pepper

2 tablespoons vegetable oil

2 pounds lamb stew meat

6 new potatoes (1 1/4 pounds), cubed

1/4 cup Dijon mustard

1/2 teaspoon grated lemon peel

1 tablespoon lemon juice

2 teaspoons chopped fresh or 1/2 teaspoon dried rosemary leaves

2 cloves garlic, finely chopped

1 can (14 1/2 ounces) ready-to-serve beef broth

1 package (10 ounces) frozen green peas, thawed

1. Mix flour, salt and pepper in resealable plastic bag. Add lamb; shake until evenly coated. Heat oil in 12-inch skillet over medium-high heat. Cook lamb in oil about 20 minutes, stirring occasionally, until brown; drain.

2. Mix lamb and remaining ingredients except peas in 3 1/2- to 6-quart slow cooker.

3. Cover and cook on low heat setting 8 to 10 hours or until lamb is tender.

4. Skim fat from juices in cooker. Stir peas into lamb mixture.

5. Cover and cook on high heat setting 10 to 15 minutes or until peas are hot.

1 Serving: Calories 300 (Calories from Fat 90); Fat 10g (Saturated 3g); Cholesterol 85mg; Sodium 940mg; Carbohydrate 30g (Dietary Fiber 5g); Protein 32g

% Daily Value: Vitamin A 2%; Vitamin C 12%; Calcium 4%; Iron 24%

Diet Exchanges: 2 Starch, 3 1/2 Lean Meat

Barbecue Beef Sandwiches

■ 12 sandwiches ■

Crowd
SIZE

SLOW COOKER:
4- to 5-quart

PREP TIME:
20 minutes

COOK TIME:
Low 7 to 8 hours

FINISHING COOK TIME:
Low 30 minutes

Ingredient Substitution

If you don't have apricot preserves, you certainly may use peach preserves or orange marmalade in its place.

Finishing Touch

For a delicious kick, spread buns with horseradish sauce. Sandwiches can be served au jus. Serve the juices left in the cooker in small bowls to dip the sandwiches in while eating to make each bite extra delicious!

3-pound beef boneless chuck roast

1 cup barbecue sauce

1/2 cup apricot preserves

1/3 cup chopped green bell pepper

1 tablespoon Dijon mustard

2 teaspoons packed brown sugar

1 small onion, sliced

12 kaiser or hamburger buns, split

1. Trim excess fat from beef. Cut beef into 4 pieces. Place beef in 4- to 5-quart slow cooker.

2. Mix remaining ingredients except buns; pour over beef. Cover and cook on low heat setting 7 to 8 hours or until beef is tender.

3. Remove beef to cutting board; cut into thin slices; return to cooker.

4. Cover and cook on low heat setting 20 to 30 minutes longer or until beef is hot. Fill buns with beef mixture.

1 Sandwich: Calories 410 (Calories from Fat 145); Fat 16g (Saturated 5g); Cholesterol 70mg; Sodium 520mg; Carbohydrate 39g (Dietary Fiber 2g); Protein 29g

% Daily Value: Vitamin A 4%; Vitamin C 8%; Calcium 6%; Iron 24%

Diet Exchanges: 2 1/2 Starch, 3 Medium-fat Meat

Barbecue Beef Sandwich ➤

Italian Beef and Green Pepper Sandwiches

■ 6 sandwiches ■

SLOW COOKER:
3 1/2- to 6-quart

PREP TIME:
15 minutes

COOK TIME:
Low 8 to 10 hours

FINISHING COOK TIME:
High 15 minutes

Betty's Success Tip

Brisket is an excellent cut to prepare in the slow cooker because the long, slow cooking ensures tenderness. Use this recipe as a guideline for preparing your favorite brisket recipe.

Ingredient Substitution

If you don't have crushed red pepper, just add a few drops of red pepper sauce when you return the beef slices to the cooker.

Finishing Touch

Sprinkle shredded mozzarella cheese and sliced ripe olives over the top of each sandwich.

2-pound fresh beef brisket

1 tablespoon vegetable oil

1 can (10 1/2 ounces) condensed beef broth

2 cloves garlic, finely chopped

1 teaspoon dried oregano leaves

1 teaspoon dried basil leaves

1/2 teaspoon salt

1/4 teaspoon pepper

1/4 teaspoon crushed red pepper

2 medium green bell peppers, cut into 1/4-inch strips

12 slices crusty Italian or French bread, each about 1 inch thick

1. Trim excess fat from beef. Heat oil in 10-inch skillet over medium-high heat. Cook beef in oil about 10 minutes, turning occasionally, until both sides are brown.

2. Place beef in 3 1/2- to 6-quart slow cooker. Mix remaining ingredients except bell peppers and bread; pour over beef.

3. Cover and cook on low heat setting 8 to 10 hours or until beef is tender.

4. Remove beef to cutting board; cut into thin slices.

5. Skim fat from beef juices in cooker if desired. Stir bell peppers into juices. Cover and cook on high heat setting 15 minutes. Return beef slices to cooker.

6. Place 2 slices of bread on each plate. Spoon beef mixture over bread.

1 Sandwich: Calories 300 (Calories from Fat 100); Fat 11g (Saturated 4g); Cholesterol 65mg; Sodium 720mg; Carbohydrate 23g (Dietary Fiber 2g); Protein 29g

% Daily Value: Vitamin A 2%; Vitamin C 30%; Calcium 4%; Iron 20%

Diet Exchanges: 1 Starch, 3 Lean Meat, 2 Vegetable

Sloppy Joes

■ *24 sandwiches* ■

SLOW COOKER:
3 1/2- to 6-quart

PREP TIME:
15 minutes

COOK TIME:
Low 7 to 9 hours
High 3 to 4 hours

Betty's Success Tip

Next time you're asked to bring something to one of your kid's events, bring Sloppy Joes. Kids love them. And you can keep the sandwich filling warm in the cooker for a couple of hours. Just be sure to stir it occasionally so that it doesn't start to get too brown around the edges.

Ingredient Substitution

Stir 1 cup drained sauerkraut into the mixture before serving. It will add a nice flavor twist, and no one will guess the "secret ingredient."

Serving Suggestion

You can serve this tasty beef mixture over hot cooked rice or pasta rather than using as a sandwich filling. Or spoon it over tortilla chips and top each serving with shredded lettuce and shredded cheese.

3 pounds ground beef

1 large onion, coarsely chopped (1 cup)

3/4 cup chopped celery

1 cup barbecue sauce

1 can (26 1/2 ounces) sloppy joe sauce

24 hamburger buns

1. Cook beef and onion in Dutch oven over medium heat, stirring occasionally, until beef is brown; drain.

2. Mix beef mixture and remaining ingredients except buns in 3 1/2- to 6-quart slow cooker.

3. Cover and cook on low heat setting 7 to 9 hours (or high heat setting 3 to 4 hours) or until vegetables are tender.

4. Uncover and cook on high heat setting until desired consistency. Stir well before serving. Fill buns with beef mixture.

1 Sandwich: Calories 155 (Calories from Fat 80); Fat 9g (Saturated 3g); Cholesterol 30mg; Sodium 270mg; Carbohydrate 8g (Dietary Fiber 1g); Protein 11g

% Daily Value: Vitamin A 2%; Vitamin C 4%; Calcium 2%; Iron 6%

Diet Exchanges: 1 High-Fat Meat, 2 Vegetable

Ginger-Orange Beef Pita Sandwiches

■ *6 sandwiches* ■

SLOW COOKER:
3 1/2- to 6-quart

PREP TIME:
25 minutes

COOK TIME:
Low 4 to 6 hours

FINISHING COOK TIME:
Low 15 minutes

Betty's Success Tip

To peel or not to peel ginger-root—that is the question. The great thing is, you can do either! Plus, if you would rather not spend the extra couple of minutes finely chopping the gingerroot, use a grater instead. Grate against the fibrous strings on the narrow ends of the gingerroot instead of the wider flat side. You can also see the fibers when you slice off a piece of gingerroot.

Serving Suggestion

This gingery beef mixture makes a fabulous sandwich, and it also makes a fabulous dinner when served with hot cooked basmati or jasmine rice and chutney. Finish the dinner with a cup of steaming tea and a bowl of coconut pudding.

1 pound beef boneless round steak

1 medium red onion, cut into eighths

1 medium orange bell pepper, cut into 1-inch pieces (1 1/2 cups)

1 medium jicama, peeled and cut into julienne strips (1 1/2 cups)

1 tablespoon grated orange peel

1/3 cup orange juice

1 teaspoon finely chopped gingerroot

1/2 teaspoon salt

1 package (6 ounces) frozen snap pea pods, thawed

3 pita breads (6 inches in diameter), cut in half to form pockets

Golden Fruit Chutney (page 177) or other chutney, if desired

1. Trim excess fat from beef. Cut beef lengthwise into 2-inch strips. Cut strips crosswise into 1/8-inch slices.

2. Place beef, onion, bell pepper and jicama in 3 1/2- to 6-quart slow cooker. Mix orange peel, orange juice, gingerroot and salt; pour over beef and vegetables.

3. Cover and cook on low heat setting 4 to 6 hours or until beef is tender.

4. Stir in snap pea pods. Cover and cook on low heat setting about 15 minutes or until pea pods are crisp-tender.

5. Spoon beef mixture into pita breads. Serve with Golden Fruit Chutney.

1 Sandwich: Calories 195 (Calories from Fat 25); Fat 3g (Saturated 1g); Cholesterol 35mg; Sodium 370mg; Carbohydrate 31g (Dietary Fiber 7g); Protein 18g

% Daily Value: Vitamin A 2%; Vitamin C 80%; Calcium 6%; Iron 18%

Diet Exchanges: 2 1/2 Very Lean Meat, 2 Fruit

Bratwurst and Sauerkraut

■ *6 sandwiches* ■

SLOW COOKER:
3 1/2- to 6-quart

PREP TIME:
5 minutes

COOK TIME:
Low 4 to 5 hours

4 fully cooked bratwurst (about 4 ounces each), cut into 1/2-inch slices

2 cans (14 1/2 ounces each) sauerkraut, drained

1/3 cup packed brown sugar

6 hot dog or bratwurst buns

1. Mix all ingredients except buns in 3 1/2- to 6-quart slow cooker.

2. Cover and cook on low heat setting 4 to 5 hours.

3. Fill buns with bratwurst mixture.

1 Sandwich: Calories 450 (Calories from Fat 215); Fat 24g (Saturated 8g); Cholesterol 45mg; Sodium 2090mg; Carbohydrate 48g (Dietary Fiber 5g); Protein 15g

% Daily Value: Vitamin A 0%; Vitamin C 18%; Calcium 14%; Iron 26%

Diet Exchanges: 2 Starch, 1 High-Fat Meat, 3 Vegetable, 3 Fat

Betty's Success Tip

Check that the brats you buy are fully cooked rather than fresh. The juice that would be released from fresh brats during cooking would add too much liquid to the mixture. If you find sauerkraut to be too salty, rinse it in a strainer under cold water to remove some of the saltiness.

Ingredient Substitution

To add that something special to this dish, stir in 1/4 teaspoon caraway seed with the other ingredients. The spicy, aromatic seed comes from an herb of the parsley family.

Finishing Touch

Chopped raw onions are good with sauerkraut and brats, so be sure there is plenty ready to spoon into this sandwich. And remember to pass the mustard—either the All-American yellow mustard or a spicier coarse-ground one.

Sweet and Saucy Ham Sandwiches

■ *12 sandwiches* ■

SLOW COOKER:
3 1/2- to 6-quart

PREP TIME:
15 minutes

COOK TIME:
Low 3 to 4 hours

FINISHING COOK TIME:
High 15 minutes

Betty's Success Tip

If you have a food processor, use it to finely chop the ham instead of grinding it. Or to save time, ask your butcher to grind it for you.

Ingredient Substitution

You can use your kids' favorite—bologna—instead of the ham. Find a 1 1/2-pound piece at the deli. If you don't have any instant minced onion on your spice rack, use 1/4 cup finely chopped onion.

Serving Suggestion

Complement the sweet-and-sour flavor of this ham filling by serving fresh fruit with the sandwiches. Arrange big, juicy red strawberries, cubes or balls of honeydew melon and cantaloupe, papaya slices and chunks of pineapple on a platter. Tuck a bowl of toasted coconut in the center of the platter to sprinkle on the fruit.

1 1/2 pounds fully cooked smoked ham, ground (4 cups)

1 cup packed brown sugar

1/2 cup Dijon mustard

1/4 cup chopped green bell pepper

1 tablespoon instant minced onion

1 can (20 ounces) crushed pineapple in juice, undrained

12 hamburger buns

1. Mix all ingredients except buns in 3 1/2- to 6-quart slow cooker.

2. Cover and cook on low heat setting 3 to 4 hours.

3. Uncover and cook on high heat setting about 15 minutes or until desired consistency. Stir well before serving. Fill buns with ham mixture.

1 Sandwich: Calories 325 (Calories from Fat 70); Fat 8g (Saturated 2g); Cholesterol 35mg; Sodium 1230mg; Carbohydrate 48g (Dietary Fiber 2g); Protein 17g

% Daily Value: Vitamin A 0%; Vitamin C 4%; Calcium 10%; Iron 16%

Diet Exchanges: 1 Starch, 2 Lean Meat, 1 Vegetable, 2 Fruit

Poultry Main Dishes

◄ *Thai Chicken (page 116)*

Chicken Stroganoff Pot Pie

■ *4 servings* ■

SLOW COOKER:
3 1/2- to 6-quart

PREP TIME:
20 minutes

COOK TIME:
Low 4 hours

FINISHING COOK TIME:
High 1 hour 10 minutes

Betty's Success Tip

A bag of frozen vegetables for stew—potatoes, carrots, onions and peas—are really handy for this recipe. The size the vegetables are cut varies from brand to brand. The good news is that both the small and medium size pieces of vegetables all were done by the end of the cooking time.

Ingredient Substitution

If you like, you can use a 1-ounce envelope of beef stroganoff mix instead of chicken gravy. The sauce will have slightly more sour cream flavor.

Serving Suggestion

What's so great about a pot pie is that it is a complete meal—chicken, vegetables and bread—all in one. Add a little crispness and color to the meal by serving a leafy green salad. Toss a bag of romaine salad greens with a drained can of mandarin orange segments and your favorite poppy seed dressing. Sprinkle each serving with some toasted sliced almonds.

1 envelope (0.87 to 1.2-ounces) chicken gravy mix

1 can (10 1/2 ounces) condensed chicken broth

1 pound skinless, boneless chicken breasts, cut into 1-inch pieces

1 bag (16 ounces) frozen stew vegetables, thawed and drained

1 jar (4 ounces) sliced mushrooms, drained

1/2 cup sour cream

1 tablespoon all-purpose flour

1 1/2 cups Bisquick Original or Reduced Fat baking mix

4 medium green onions, chopped (1/4 cup)

1/2 cup milk

1 cup frozen green peas, thawed

1. Mix gravy mix and broth in 3 1/2- to 6-quart slow cooker until smooth. Stir in chicken, stew vegetables and mushrooms.

2. Cover and cook on low heat setting about 4 hours or until chicken is tender.

3. Mix sour cream and flour. Stir sour cream mixture into chicken mixture. Cover and cook on high heat setting 20 minutes.

4. Mix baking mix and onions; stir in milk just until moistened. Stir in peas. Drop dough by rounded tablespoonfuls onto chicken-vegetable mixture.

5. Cover and cook on high heat setting 45 to 50 minutes or until toothpick inserted in center of topping comes out clean. Serve immediately.

1 Serving: Calories 535 (Calories from Fat 155); Fat 17g (Saturated 7g); Cholesterol 95mg; Sodium 2100mg; Carbohydrate 56g (Dietary Fiber 5g); Protein 45g

% Daily Value: Vitamin A 42%; Vitamin C 6%; Calcium 18%; Iron 20%

Diet Exchanges: 3 Starch, 4 Lean Meat, 2 Vegetable, 1 Fat

Creamy Chicken and Wild Rice

■ 6 servings ■

SLOW COOKER:
2- to 3 1/2-quart

PREP TIME:
10 minutes

COOK TIME:
Low 5 to 6 hours

STAND TIME:
15 minutes

Betty's Success Tip

This is the perfect recipe to have all the ingredients on hand. Cut the chicken into 1-inch pieces before storing in the freezer. Just defrost the chicken in the microwave and pop everything in your slow cooker—what could be easier?

Finishing Touch

The wonderful flavors of Parmesan cheese and toasted almonds are a natural with wild rice and chicken.

1 package (8.25 ounces) skillet-dinner mix for mushroom and wild rice

1 pound skinless, boneless chicken breasts, cut into 1-inch pieces

1 can (14 1/2 ounces) ready-to-serve chicken broth

1 can (12 ounces) evaporated milk

1/2 cup water

2 tablespoons margarine or butter, melted

2 tablespoons instant chopped onion

1. Mix uncooked rice and sauce mix (from dinner mix) and remaining ingredients in 2- to 3 1/2-quart slow cooker.

2. Cover and cook on low heat setting 5 to 6 hours or until rice is tender.

3. Stir mixture. Cover and let stand about 15 minutes or until thickened and desired consistency.

1 Serving: Calories 330 (Calories from Fat 100); Fat 11g (Saturated 3g); Cholesterol 80mg; Sodium 1250mg; Carbohydrate 33g (Dietary Fiber 2g); Protein 27g

% Daily Value: Vitamin A 10%; Vitamin C 2%; Calcium 20%; Iron 8%

Diet Exchanges: 2 Starch, 3 Lean Meat, 1 Vegetable

Italian Sun-Dried Tomato Chicken Breasts

■ *4 servings* ■

SLOW COOKER:
2- to 4 1/2-quart

PREP TIME:
15 minutes

COOK TIME:
Low 8 to 9 hours

Betty's Success Tip

The best way to cut sun-dried tomato halves into julienne strips is to use a kitchen scissors. You purchased bulk sun-dried tomatoes? You will need about 30 tomato halves for a cup of julienne strips.

Serving Suggestion

Polenta, an Italian cornmeal favorite, is the perfect mate for this flavorful chicken dish. Either make your favorite polenta recipe, or purchase the polenta found in your supermarket's refrigerated-foods section of the produce area. Sauté thick slices of polenta in olive oil until golden brown on both sides. Serve with hot, whole green beans.

Finishing Touch

To make this a real Italian treat, sprinkle with shredded Parmesan cheese and about 1/2 cup toasted pine nuts. To toast the nuts, cook them in a heavy skillet over medium-low heat about 5 minutes, stirring frequently until they begin to brown. Then stir them constantly until they are golden brown and you can smell that wonderful nutty aroma.

1 package (3 ounces) sun-dried tomatoes (not oil-packed), cut into julienne strips (about 1 cup)

4 skinless, boneless chicken breast halves (about 1 pound)

1/3 cup coarsely chopped fresh or 1 tablespoon dried basil leaves

1 package (8 ounces) sliced mushrooms (3 cups)

1 can (2 1/4 ounces) sliced ripe olives, rinsed and drained

1. Place all ingredients in 2- to 4 1/2-quart slow cooker.

2. Cover and cook on low heat setting 8 to 9 hours or until juice of chicken is no longer pink when centers of thickest pieces are cut.

1 Serving: Calories 225 (Calories from Fat 55); Fat 6g (Saturated 1g); Cholesterol 75mg; Sodium 650mg; Carbohydrate 16g (Dietary Fiber 4g); Protein 31g

% Daily Value: Vitamin A 4%; Vitamin C 8%; Calcium 6%; Iron 22%

Diet Exchanges: 4 Very Lean Meat, 3 Vegetable

Mexican Chicken with Green Chili Rice

■ *4 servings* ■

SLOW COOKER:
3 1/2- to 6-quart

PREP TIME:
15 minutes

COOK TIME:
Low 7 to 8 hours

Ingredient Substitution

Cumin, a tiny seed the size and shape of a caraway seed, is the dried fruit of the parsley family. This aromatic spice is a popular seasoning for Mexican cooking and is also one of the spices in chili powder. You can use 1/4 teaspoon chili powder to replace the ground cumin in this chicken dish.

Serving Suggestion

A fresh orange salad would be nice to serve with this chicken and rice dish. Arrange slices of oranges on romaine or other salad greens. Top with a big spoonful of guacamole and a sprinkle of toasted slivered almonds.

Finishing Touch

If you like your bell pepper with a bit of crunch, add it to the mixture for the last 15 minutes of cooking. Uncover and cook on high heat setting about 15 minutes or until pepper is crisp-tender.

1 medium butternut squash, peeled and cut into 2-inch pieces

1 medium green bell pepper, cut into 1-inch pieces

4 skinless, boneless chicken breast halves (about 1 pound), each cut into 3 pieces

1 can (14 1/2 ounces) stewed tomatoes, undrained

1/2 cup salsa

1/4 cup raisins

1/4 teaspoon ground cinnamon

1/4 teaspoon ground cumin

3 cups hot cooked rice, for serving

1 can (4 ounces) chopped green chilies, drained

1. Layer squash, bell pepper and chicken in 3 1/2- to 6-quart slow cooker. Mix tomatoes, salsa, raisins, cinnamon and cumin; pour over chicken mixture.

2. Cover and cook on low heat setting 7 to 8 hours or until squash is tender and juice of chicken is no longer pink when centers of thickest pieces are cut.

3. Mix rice and chilies.

4. Remove chicken and vegetables from cooker, using slotted spoon. Serve on rice. Stir sauce in cooker; spoon over chicken and vegetables.

1 Serving: Calories 400 (Calories from Fat 45); Fat 5g (Saturated 1g); Cholesterol 75mg; Sodium 490mg; Carbohydrate 61g (Dietary Fiber 4g); Protein 32g

% Daily Value: Vitamin A 60%; Vitamin C 62%; Calcium 10%; Iron 22%

Diet Exchanges: 3 Starch, 2 Lean Meat, 3 Vegetable

Mango Chutney Chicken Curry

■ 4 servings ■

SLOW COOKER:
3 1/2- to 4-quart

PREP TIME:
20 minutes

COOK TIME:
Low 6 to 7 hours

Ingredient Substitution

Chutney is a spicy mixture of fruit, vinegar, sugar and spices. It can vary in texture from chunky to smooth and in spiciness from mild to hot. We liked the sweetness of the mango chutney, but try the Golden Fruit Chutney on page 177 or your favorite chutney in this curried delight.

Finishing Touch

Serve small bowls of traditional curry dish toppers, such as toasted shredded coconut, chopped peanuts and raisins. The saltiness of the peanuts and the sweetness of the coconut and raisins enhance the flavors of the curry powder and chutney. Serve additional mango chutney to spoon alongside the chicken and rice.

4 skinless, bone-in chicken breast halves (about 7 ounces each)

1 can (15 to 16 ounces) garbanzo beans, rinsed and drained

1 small onion, thinly sliced

1 small red bell pepper, chopped (1/2 cup)

1 cup snap pea pods

3/4 cup water

2 tablespoons cornstarch

1 1/2 teaspoons curry powder

1/4 teaspoon salt

1/4 teaspoon pepper

1 jar (9 ounces) mango chutney

4 cups hot cooked rice or couscous, for serving

1. Layer chicken, beans, onion, bell pepper and pea pods in 3 1/2- to 4-quart slow cooker. Mix remaining ingredients except rice; pour into cooker.

2. Cover and cook on low heat setting 6 to 7 hours or until vegetables are tender and juice of chicken is no longer pink when centers of thickest pieces are cut.

3. Serve chicken mixture over rice.

1 Serving: Calories 600 (Calories from Fat 65); Fat 7g (Saturated 2g); Cholesterol 75mg; Sodium 410mg; Carbohydrate 103g (Dietary Fiber 11g); Protein 42g

% Daily Value: Vitamin A 12%; Vitamin C 42%; Calcium 10%; Iron 38%

Diet Exchanges: 3 Starch, 4 Very Lean Meat, 2 Vegetable, 3 Fruit

Herbed Chicken and Stuffing Supper

■ 6 servings ■

SLOW COOKER:
5- to 6-quart

PREP TIME:
20 minutes

COOK TIME:
Low 4 to 6 hours

FINISHING COOK TIME:
Low 15 to 20 minutes

3 pounds bone-in chicken pieces, skin removed

1 can (10 3/4 ounces) condensed cream of chicken with herbs soup

4 sweet potatoes or yams, peeled and cut into 1/2-inch slices

1 package (6 ounces) stuffing mix for chicken

1 1/4 cups water

1/4 cup margarine or butter, melted

1 cup frozen (thawed) cut green beans

1. Place chicken in 5- to 6-quart slow cooker. Spoon soup over chicken. Top with sweet potatoes. Mix stuffing mix, water and margarine; spoon over sweet potatoes.

2. Cover and cook on low heat setting 4 to 6 hours or until potatoes are tender and juice of chicken is no longer pink when centers of thickest pieces are cut.

3. Sprinkle green beans over stuffing. Cover and cook on low heat setting 15 to 20 minutes or until beans are tender.

1 Serving: Calories 520 (Calories from Fat 205); Fat 23g (Saturated 6g); Cholesterol 150mg; Sodium 740mg; Carbohydrate 30g (Dietary Fiber 3g); Protein 51g

% Daily Value: Vitamin A 100%; Vitamin C 16%; Calcium 6%; Iron 16%

Diet Exchanges: 2 Starch, 6 1/2 Lean Meat

Betty's Success Tip

The stuffing mix for chicken is the already-flavored bread crumb mixture that comes in a box. All the seasoning are included, and you just add the water and the butter—it's that easy! You can use your family's favorite chicken pieces, such as legs, thighs, breasts or a mixture of all three, so everyone gets his or her favorite "pick of the day."

Ingredient Substitution

The herbs in the cream of chicken soup make a nicely seasoned one-dish meal. You also can use your favorite cream soup, such as golden onion or broccoli.

Finishing Touch

We like to add the green beans at the end of the cooking time so that they keep their green color and have more texture. But you don't have to; you can add the green beans with the sweet potatoes, but they will be softer in texture and a lighter green color.

Chicken in Red Wine

■ 8 servings ■

SLOW COOKER:
5- to 6-quart

PREP TIME:
20 minutes

COOK TIME:
Low 8 to 10 hours
High 3 to 5 hours

FINISHING COOK TIME:
High 30 minutes

Betty's Success Tip

This robust chicken dish, known as Coq au Vin in France, gets its wonderful flavor and rich color from the red wine and bacon. It is usually prepared with bone-in chicken pieces, but we found that the boneless chicken thighs work the best in the slow cooker. The chicken becomes very tender and can fall apart when being served.

Ingredient Substitution

If you prefer not to use red wine, you still can make a delicious chicken dish your family will love. Just increase the chicken broth to 2 cups and leave out the wine.

Serving Suggestion

Be sure to serve this saucy dish in shallow soup bowls. Parsleyed potatoes are the traditional accompaniment to this hearty, flavorful dish, and you can serve them right in the bowl with the chicken. Chunks of a crusty bread are always nice for soaking up all the wine-flavored sauce left in the bowl!

8 skinless, boneless chicken thighs (about 1 1/2 pounds)

1 bag (16 ounces) baby-cut carrots

8 ounces tiny pearl onions

6 slices bacon, cooked and crumbled

1 teaspoon salt

1/4 teaspoon pepper

2 cloves garlic, finely chopped

Bouquet Garni (below)

1 1/4 cups dry red wine

3/4 cup chicken broth

1 pound small whole button mushrooms

2 tablespoons all-purpose flour

2 tablespoons cold water

1. Place chicken in 5- to 6-quart slow cooker. Add remaining ingredients except mushrooms, flour and water.

2. Cover and cook on low heat setting 8 to 10 hours (or high heat setting 3 to 5 hours) or until juice of chicken is no longer pink when centers of thickest pieces are cut.

3. Remove any fat from surface. Remove Bouquet Garni. Stir in mushrooms. Mix flour and water; stir into chicken mixture.

4. Cover and cook on high heat setting about 30 minutes or until mixture is thickened.

Bouquet Garni

Tie 4 sprigs parsley, 2 bay leaves and 1 teaspoon dried thyme leaves in cheese cloth bag or place in tea ball.

1 Serving: Calories 190 (Calories from Fat 70); Fat 8g (Saturated 3g); Cholesterol 45mg; Sodium 530mg; Carbohydrate 13g (Dietary Fiber 3g); Protein 19g

% Daily Value: Vitamin A 88%; Vitamin C 6%; Calcium 4%; Iron 14%

Diet Exchanges: 3 Lean Meat, 3 Vegetable

Thai Chicken

■ *4 servings* ■

SLOW COOKER:
3 1/2- to 6-quart

PREP TIME:
15 minutes

COOK TIME:
Low 8 to 9 hours

FINISHING COOK TIME:
50 minutes

8 chicken thighs (about 2 pounds), skin removed

3/4 cup hot salsa

1/4 cup peanut butter

2 tablespoons lime juice

1 tablespoon soy sauce

1 teaspoon grated fresh gingerroot

1/4 cup chopped peanuts

2 tablespoons chopped fresh cilantro

1. Place chicken in 3 1/2- to 6-quart slow cooker. Mix remaining ingredients except peanuts and cilantro; pour over chicken.

2. Cover and cook on low heat setting 8 to 9 hours or until juice of chicken is no longer pink when centers of thickest pieces are cut. Remove chicken from cooker, using slotted spoon; place on serving platter.

3. Remove fat from sauce. Pour sauce over chicken. Sprinkle with peanuts and cilantro.

1 Serving: Calories 380 (Calories from Fat 215); Fat 24g (Saturated 6g); Cholesterol 85mg; Sodium 550mg; Carbohydrate 8g (Dietary Fiber 3g); Protein 36g

% Daily Value: Vitamin A 2%; Vitamin C 10%; Calcium 6%; Iron 18%

Diet Exchanges: 4 Medium-Fat Meat, 2 Vegetable, 1 Fat

Betty's Success Tip

The flavors of peanut butter, tomato and hot chilies are a popular Thai combination. We took a shortcut and used hot salsa for the tomatoes and chilies. For an equally tasty dish with a little less kick, use a milder salsa.

Ingredient Substitution

Had that bottle of fish sauce on your shelf since the last time you cooked Thai? You can replace the soy sauce in this recipe with fish sauce for a more authentic Thai flavor. If you want to try fish sauce for the first time, look for it at an Asian-foods market or a large supermarket. It is salty like soy sauce but has a pungent, strong fish flavor.

Serving Suggestion

Complement this dish by serving it with rice that has been tossed with coconut. The coconut rice is especially good when you use the hot salsa in the chicken. Add a side of cucumber vinaigrette, and you'll have a blend of flavors and textures that will leave happy memories in your mouth!

Chicken Legs with Herbed Onion Sauce

5 servings

SLOW COOKER:
31/2- to 6-quart

PREP TIME:
15 minutes

COOK TIME:
Low 4 to 5 hours

Betty's Success Tip

Removing the skin from the chicken legs before cooking also removes some of the extra fat. This will save you the time of having to spoon that extra fat off the top of the sauce before you serve it.

Ingredient Substitution

Those fresh little pearl onions can be time consuming to peel, so using the frozen thawed ones saves you a lot of time. If you don't have pearl onions in the freezer, you can slice and use a large yellow or white onion.

Finishing Touch

Serve all that wonderfully flavored sauce spooned over the chicken legs. Tuck a perky sprig of fresh tarragon or rosemary next to the chicken, or sprinkle a little chopped fresh parsley over the top for that special touch.

10 chicken drumsticks (about 2 pounds), skin removed

2 cups frozen (thawed) pearl onions

1/4 cup dry white wine or chicken broth

1/4 cup canned evaporated milk

2 tablespoons chopped fresh parsley or 2 teaspoons parsley flakes

1 teaspoon dried tarragon leaves

1/4 teaspoon salt

1/4 teaspoon dried rosemary leaves, crumbled

1 can (10 3/4 ounces) condensed cream of chicken soup

1. Place chicken in 3 1/2- to 6-quart slow cooker. Mix remaining ingredients; pour over chicken.

2. Cover and cook on low heat setting 4 to 5 hours or until juice of chicken is no longer pink when centers of thickest pieces are cut.

1 Serving: Calories 230 (Calories from Fat 70); Fat 8g (Saturated 3g); Cholesterol 105mg; Sodium 640mg; Carbohydrate 11g (Dietary Fiber 1g); Protein 29g

% Daily Value: Vitamin A 4%; Vitamin C 4%; Calcium 8%; Iron 16%

Diet Exchanges: 3 1/2 Very Lean Meat, 2 Vegetable, 1 Fat

Moroccan Chicken

■ 4 servings ■

SLOW COOKER:
5- to 6-quart

PREP TIME:
15 minutes

COOK TIME:
Low 4 to 5 hours

FINISHING COOK TIME:
High 15 minutes

Ingredient Substitution

Turmeric is the ground root of a tropical plant. It has a slightly pungent gingery flavor and an intense yellow-orange color. If you prefer not to use turmeric, you may want to add a dash of ground ginger instead. The color will be a little bit lighter, but the flavor will be just as good!

Serving Suggestion

Couscous is as fun to say as it is to serve! Make about 3 cups of couscous to go with these saucy chicken legs. It only takes minutes to prepare and will soak up all that wonderful sauce that is spooned over the chicken. For a flavor twist that goes great with this dish, cook the couscous in pineapple juice instead of water.

8 chicken drumsticks (about 1 1/2 pounds), skin removed

1 can (8 ounces) pineapple tidbits or chunks in juice, undrained

1 large onion, chopped (1 cup)

2 cloves garlic, finely chopped

2 tablespoons lemon juice

1 teaspoon salt

1 teaspoon dried marjoram leaves

3/4 teaspoon crushed red pepper

1/4 teaspoon ground turmeric

1 tablespoon cornstarch

1 tablespoon cold water

1/4 cup sliced pimiento-stuffed olives

1 tablespoon chopped fresh parsley

1. Place chicken in 5- to 6-quart slow cooker. Mix pineapple, onion, garlic, lemon juice, salt, marjoram, red pepper and turmeric; pour over chicken.

2. Cover and cook on low heat setting 4 to 5 hours or until juice of chicken is no longer pink when centers of thickest pieces are cut. Remove chicken from cooker, using slotted spoon; place in serving dish. Cover to keep warm.

3. Remove fat from sauce. Mix cornstarch and water; stir into sauce.

4. Cover and cook on high heat setting about 15 minutes or until thickened. Stir in olives.

5. Pour sauce over chicken. Sprinkle with parsley.

1 Serving: Calories 210 (Calories from Fat 55); Fat 6g (Saturated 2g); Cholesterol 100mg; Sodium 960mg; Carbohydrate 15g (Dietary Fiber 2g); Protein 26g

% Daily Value: Vitamin A 2%; Vitamin C 8%; Calcium 4%; Iron 16%

Diet Exchanges: 4 Very Lean Meat, 1 Fruit

Moroccan Chicken ➤

Herbed Turkey and Wild Rice Casserole

■ *6 servings* ■

SLOW COOKER:
3 1/2- to 6-quart

PREP TIME:
15 minutes

STARTING COOK TIME:
High 30 minutes

COOK TIME:
Low 6 to 7 hours

Betty's Success Tip

Take a few minutes to cook the bacon and brown the turkey and vegetables before adding them to the slow cooker. You'll get the great bacon flavor but not the extra fat because it is drained off. Don't add the vegetables until the turkey is browned because their moisture will cook out and simmer the turkey, keeping it from turning a nice golden brown.

Ingredient Substitution

Are you watching your sodium intake? Use the reduced-sodium chicken broth and cream of chicken soup to save 500 milligrams of sodium for each serving.

6 slices bacon, cut into 1/2-inch pieces

1 pound turkey breast tenderloins, cut into 3/4-inch pieces

1 medium onion, chopped (1/2 cup)

1 medium carrot, sliced (1/2 cup)

1 medium stalk celery, sliced (1/2 cup)

2 cans (14 1/2 ounces each) ready-to-serve chicken broth

1 can (10 3/4 ounces) condensed cream of chicken soup

1/4 teaspoon dried marjoram leaves

1/8 teaspoon pepper

1 1/4 cups uncooked wild rice, rinsed and drained

1. Cook bacon in 10-inch skillet over medium heat, stirring occasionally, until crisp. Stir in turkey. Cook 3 to 5 minutes, stirring occasionally, until turkey is brown. Stir in onion, carrot and celery. Cook 2 minutes, stirring occasionally; drain.

2. Beat 1 can of the broth and the soup in 3 1/2- to 6-quart slow cooker, using wire whisk, until smooth. Stir in remaining can of broth, the marjoram and pepper. Stir in turkey mixture and wild rice.

3. Cover and cook on high heat setting 30 minutes.

4. Reduce heat to low setting. Cook 6 to 7 hours or until rice is tender and liquid is absorbed.

1 Serving: Calories 320 (Calories from Fat 70); Fat 8g (Saturated 3g); Cholesterol 60mg; Sodium 1140mg; Carbohydrate 36g (Dietary Fiber 3g); Protein 29g

% Daily Value: Vitamin A 18%; Vitamin C 2%; Calcium 2%; Iron 14%

Diet Exchanges: 2 Starch, 3 Very Lean Meat, 1 Vegetable, 1 Fat

Herbed Turkey and Wild Rice Casserole ➤

Turkey Drumsticks with Plum Sauce

■ *4 servings* ■

SLOW COOKER:
5- to 6-quart

PREP TIME:
10 minutes

COOK TIME:
Low 8 to 10 hours

FINISHING COOK TIME:
High 15 to 20 minutes

4 turkey drumsticks (2 1/2 to 3 pounds), skin removed

1/2 teaspoon salt

1/4 teaspoon pepper

2/3 cup plum sauce

1/3 cup sliced green onions

1 tablespoon soy sauce

1 tablespoon cornstarch

1 tablespoon cold water

3 cups hot cooked rice, for serving

1. Sprinkle turkey with salt and pepper. Place turkey in 5- to 6-quart slow cooker. Mix plum sauce, onions and soy sauce; pour over turkey.

2. Cover and cook on low heat setting 8 to 10 hours or until juice of turkey is no longer pink when centers of thickest pieces are cut.

3. Remove turkey from cooker. Cover with aluminum foil to keep warm.

4. Remove any fat from sauce. Mix cornstarch and water; stir into sauce.

5. Cover and cook on high heat setting 15 to 20 minutes or until sauce has thickened. Cut turkey from drumsticks. Serve with sauce and rice.

1 Serving: Calories 510 (Calories from Fat 80); Fat 9g (Saturated 3g); Cholesterol 210mg; Sodium 680mg; Carbohydrate 50g (Dietary Fiber 1g); Protein 58g

% Daily Value: Vitamin A 0%; Vitamin C 2%; Calcium 8%; Iron 36%

Diet Exchanges: 3 Starch, 7 Very Lean Meat, 1 Vegetable

Betty's Success Tip

Take a few minutes to remove the skin before cooking the drumsticks. First, less fat will form on top of the sauce during cooking. Second, the skin would not become golden brown because it will be simmering in the sauce. Third, the flavor of the plum sauce will cling to the turkey meat instead of to the skin.

Ingredient Substitution

Plum sauce is a sweet-and-sour sauce made from plums, apricots, sugar and seasonings. You can find it in the Asian-foods section of the supermarket or at an Asian grocery store. If plum sauce isn't available, use apricot or cherry preserves and it still will be delicious!

Serving Suggestion

Keep to the Asian theme by serving this plum-good turkey with crisply cooked pea pods. A fresh salad of assorted melon—cantaloupe, honeydew and watermelon—drizzled lightly with your favorite fruit salad dressing makes a light yet satisfying meal.

Turkey Drumsticks with Plum Sauce ➤

Turkey Breast Stuffed with Wild Rice and Cranberries

■ *10 servings* ■

SLOW COOKER:
3 1/2- to 6-quart

PREP TIME:
25 minutes

COOK TIME:
Low 8 to 9 hours

What a Great Idea...
for Leftovers

Turkey Stuffing Burgers (page 126) and Layered Turkey and Sweet Potato Casserole (page 127) are two yummy ways for using that extra-cooked turkey and stuffing. Your family will welcome having "leftovers!"

Remove stuffing from turkey. Chop turkey and mix with stuffing. Divide mixture among freezer or refrigerator containers, placing 2 cups in each. Cover and refrigerate up to 4 days or freeze up to 4 months. To thaw frozen turkey mixture, place container in refrigerator about 8 hours.

4 cups cooked wild rice

3/4 cup finely chopped onion

1/2 cup dried cranberries

1/3 cup slivered almonds

2 medium peeled or unpeeled cooking apples, coarsely chopped (2 cups)

4- to 5-pound boneless whole turkey breast, thawed if frozen

1. Mix all ingredients except turkey. Cut turkey into slices at 1-inch intervals about three-fourths of the way through, forming deep pockets.

2. Place turkey in 3 1/2- to 6-quart slow cooker. Stuff pockets with wild rice mixture. Place remaining rice mixture around edge of cooker.

3. Cover and cook on low heat setting 8 to 9 hours or until turkey is no longer pink in center.

1 Serving: Calories 400 (Calories from Fat 125); Fat 14g (Saturated 3g); Cholesterol 115mg; Sodium 100mg; Carbohydrate 26g (Dietary Fiber 4g); Protein 47g

% Daily Value: Vitamin A 4%; Vitamin C 6%; Calcium 4%; Iron 12%

Diet Exchanges: 1 Starch, 6 Very Lean Meat, 2 Vegetable, 1 Fat

what a
Great Idea...

Turkey Breast Stuffed with Wild Rice and Cranberries ➤

for Leftovers

What a Great Idea ... for Leftovers!

Use extra Turkey Breast Stuffed with Wild Rice and Cranberries (page 124) to make healthy turkey burgers or a casserole featuring sweet potatoes that bursts with homemade goodness.

Turkey Stuffing Burgers

PREP TIME: 10 minutes • COOK TIME: 12 minutes

■ *4 servings* ■

1 container (2 cups) Turkey Breast Stuffed with Wild Rice and Cranberries (page 124), thawed if frozen

1 egg, slightly beaten

1/2 cup saltine cracker crumbs

2 tablespoons margarine or butter

4 hamburger buns, split

1 cup shredded lettuce

2 medium tomatoes, sliced

Whole berry cranberry sauce, if desired

1. Mix turkey mixture and egg; shape into 4 patties. Coat with cracker crumbs.

2. Melt margarine in 12-inch skillet over medium heat. Cook patties in margarine 4 to 5 minutes on each side or until hot and golden brown.

3. Serve patties on buns topped with lettuce, tomatoes and cranberry sauce.

1 Serving: Calories 375 (Calories from Fat 115); Fat 13g (Saturated 3g); Cholesterol 100mg; Sodium 460mg; Carbohydrate 43g (Dietary Fiber 5g); Protein 26g

% Daily Value: Vitamin A 14%; Vitamin C 14%; Calcium 8%; Iron 18%

Diet Exchanges: 2 Starch, 2 Medium-Fat Meat, 3 Vegetable

Layered Turkey and Sweet Potato Casserole

Prep Time: 10 minutes • Bake Time: 30 minutes

■ *4 servings* ■

1 can (18 ounces) vacuum-pack sweet potatoes

1 container (2 cups) Turkey Breast Stuffed with Wild Rice and Cranberries (page 124), thawed if frozen

1 can (10 3/4 ounces) condensed cream of chicken soup

1/3 cup milk

1/4 cup slivered almonds, toasted (page 152), if desired

1. Heat oven to 350°. Grease 2-quart casserole.

2. Mash sweet potatoes with fork; spread in casserole. Spread turkey mixture over sweet potatoes.

3. Mix soup and milk; spoon over turkey mixture. Sprinkle with almonds.

4. Bake uncovered about 30 minutes or until hot in center.

1 Serving: Calories 385 (Calories from Fat 90); Fat 10g (Saturated 2g); Cholesterol 60mg; Sodium 650mg; Carbohydrate 53g (Dietary Fiber 6g); Protein 27g

% Daily Value: Vitamin A 96%; Vitamin C 14%; Calcium 8%; Iron 16%

Diet Exchanges: 3 Starch, 2 Lean Meat, 1 Vegetable, 1/2 Fat

Turkey Breast with Bulgur and Feta Cheese

■ *6 servings* ■

SLOW COOKER:
3 1/2- to 6-quart

PREP TIME:
20 minutes

COOK TIME:
Low 4 to 5 hours

Betty's Success Tip

Sometimes the only place you can find the size turkey breast you need is in the freezer section. The best way to thaw a frozen turkey breast is to place it in the refrigerator. Allow about 24 hours for the 2- to 2 1/2-pound turkey breast in this recipe. Forget to take the turkey out of the freezer in time to thaw in refrigerator? Use the cold-water thawing method by placing the tightly wrapped turkey breast in cold water. Allow 30 minutes per pound to thaw, and change the water often so it stays cold.

Ingredient Substitution

Kalamata olives are assertively flavored purple-black ripe olives soaked in a wine-vinegar marinade. They add a delightful flavor accent, but you also can use a drained 2 1/4-ounce can of sliced ripe olives instead.

2- to 2 1/2-pound bone-in turkey breast half, thawed if frozen

1/2 teaspoon salt

1/2 teaspoon dried oregano leaves

1 cup uncooked bulgur or cracked wheat

3 tablespoons lemon juice

1 teaspoon dried oregano leaves

1/4 teaspoon pepper

4 medium green onions, sliced (1/4 cup)

1 clove garlic, finely chopped

1 can (14 1/2 ounces) ready-to-serve chicken broth

1/4 cup pitted Kalamata or Greek olives

1/4 cup crumbled feta cheese

1. Sprinkle turkey with salt and 1/2 teaspoon oregano. Mix remaining ingredients except olives and cheese in 3 1/2- to 6-quart slow cooker. Place turkey on top.

2. Cover and cook on low heat setting 4 to 5 hours or until juice of turkey is no longer pink when center is cut. Remove turkey from cooker; cut into slices.

3. Stir olives and cheese into bulgur mixture. Serve with turkey.

1 Serving: Calories 295 (Calories from Fat 100); Fat 11g (Saturated 3g); Cholesterol 85mg; Sodium 710mg; Carbohydrate 20g (Dietary Fiber 5g); Protein 34g

% Daily Value: Vitamin A 4%; Vitamin C 2%; Calcium 6%; Iron 12%

Diet Exchanges: 1 Starch, 4 Very Lean Meat, 1 Vegetable, 1 Fat

Turkey and Vegetables with Cornmeal Dumplings

■ *6 servings* ■

SLOW COOKER:
3 1/2- to 6-quart

PREP TIME:
15 minutes

COOK TIME:
Low 8 to 10 hours

FINISHING COOK TIME:
High 35 to 45 minutes

Betty's Success Tip

Be sure the turkey thighs are tender before you mix up the dumpling dough. If the dough stands too long before adding to the top of the turkey mixture, the baking powder will start to work and the volume of the dumplings may not be as good as it should be.

Finishing Touch

Bolitas—"little balls"—or dumplings made with cornmeal and flavored with onion and thyme, are popular throughout Latin America. To add a little smoky flavor, cook and crumble 4 slices of bacon to sprinkle over the dumplings before serving.

2 turkey thighs (about 2 pounds), skin and bones removed

1 can (15 1/4 ounces) whole kernel corn, undrained

1 can (8 ounces) tomato sauce

2 tablespoons all-purpose flour

1 teaspoon chili powder

1 teaspoon salt

1/4 teaspoon pepper

Cornmeal Dumplings (below)

1 medium zucchini, sliced (2 cups)

1/4 teaspoon salt

1. Place turkey in 3 1/2- to 6-quart slow cooker. Mix corn, tomato sauce, flour, chili powder, 1 teaspoon salt and the pepper; pour over turkey.

2. Cover and cook on low heat setting 8 to 10 hours or until juice of turkey is no longer pink when center of thickest piece is cut.

3. Prepare Cornmeal Dumplings. Drop dough by spoonfuls onto hot turkey mixture. Arrange zucchini slices around dumplings; sprinkle with 1/4 teaspoon salt. Cover and cook on high heat setting 35 to 45 minutes or until toothpick inserted in center of dumplings comes out clean.

Cornmeal Dumplings

Mix 1/2 cup all-purpose flour, 1/2 cup yellow cornmeal, 1/4 cup milk, 2 tablespoons vegetable oil, 1 teaspoon baking powder, 1/4 teaspoon salt, 1/4 teaspoon ground thyme, 1 egg, and 1 small onion, finely chopped together.

1 Serving: Calories 370 (Calories from Fat 100); Fat 11g (Saturated 3g); Cholesterol 140mg; Sodium 960mg; Carbohydrate 39g (Dietary Fiber 4g); Protein 33g

% Daily Value: Vitamin A 10%; Vitamin C 12%; Calcium 10%; Iron 26%

Diet Exchanges: 2 Starch, 3 Lean Meat, 2 Vegetable

Rosemary Turkey and Sweet Potatoes

■ *6 servings* ■

SLOW COOKER:
3 1/2- to 6-quart

PREP TIME:
15 minutes

COOK TIME:
Low 8 to 10 hours

Betty's Success Tip

Potatoes sometimes take longer to cook than other vegetables or meats in a slow cooker. By putting them into the cooker first, they are in liquid during the long cooking time and will be done in the same time as the other ingredients.

Ingredient Substitution

If you're not a sweet potato lover, use 3 medium white potatoes, cut into 2-inch pieces, instead. There's no need to peel the white potatoes because the skins are nutritious and add a nice color contrast to the green beans.

3 medium sweet potatoes, peeled and cut into 2-inch pieces

1 package (10 ounces) frozen cut green beans

3 turkey thighs (about 3 pounds), skin removed

1 jar (12 ounces) home-style turkey gravy

2 tablespoons all-purpose flour

1 teaspoon parsley flakes

1/2 teaspoon dried rosemary leaves, crumbled

1/8 teaspoon pepper

1. Layer sweet potatoes, green beans and turkey in 3 1/2- to 6-quart slow cooker. Mix remaining ingredients until smooth; pour over mixture in cooker.

2. Cover and cook on low heat setting 8 to 10 hours or until juice of turkey is no longer pink when centers of thickest pieces are cut.

3. Remove turkey and vegetables from cooker, using slotted spoon. Stir sauce; serve with turkey and vegetables.

1 Serving: Calories 335 (Calories from Fat 70); Fat 8g (Saturated 3g); Cholesterol 155mg; Sodium 450mg; Carbohydrate 26g (Dietary Fiber 4g); Protein 44g

% Daily Value: Vitamin A 100%; Vitamin C 16%; Calcium 8%; Iron 26%

Diet Exchanges: 1 Starch, 5 Very Lean Meat, 2 Vegetable, 1/2 Fat

Southwestern Turkey

■ 6 servings ■

SLOW COOKER:
2 1/2- to 4-quart

PREP TIME:
15 minutes

COOK TIME:
Low 4 to 6 hours

1 tablespoon olive or vegetable oil

11/4 pounds turkey breast tenderloins, cut into 1-inch cubes

1 can (14 1/2 ounces) diced tomatoes with Mexican seasoning, undrained

1/2 medium green bell pepper, thinly sliced

1 tablespoon chili powder

2 tablespoons lime juice

1 teaspoon sugar

1/2 teaspoon salt

1. Heat oil in 12-inch skillet over medium-high heat. Cook turkey in oil 4 to 6 minutes, stirring occasionally, until brown. Place turkey in 2 1/2- to 4-quart slow cooker.

2. Mix remaining ingredients; pour over turkey.

3. Cover and cook on low heat setting 4 to 6 hours or until turkey is no longer pink in center.

Serving Suggestion

Just get home and know everyone is hungry? Make some boil-in-the-bag rice as a bed for this yummy turkey. It'll take about 15 minutes to cook. Pop some whole kernel corn into the microwave for a pleasing side dish. The next thing you know, you'll have dinner on the table before the family can ask "What's for dinner?"

Finishing Touch

Cilantro is a popular herb used in many Southwestern recipes. It has a pungent flavor and aroma with a cool, minty overtone. Sprinkle a couple tablespoons of chopped fresh cilantro over the turkey just before serving to add extra flavor to this dish.

1 Serving: Calories 125 (Calories from Fat 20); Fat 3g (Saturated 0g); Cholesterol 60mg; Sodium 350mg; Carbohydrate 5g (Dietary Fiber 1g); Protein 23g

% Daily Value: Vitamin A 8%; Vitamin C 16%; Calcium 4%; Iron 10%

Diet Exchanges: 3 Very Lean Meat, 1 Vegetable

Turkey Sausage Cassoulet

■ 4 servings ■

SLOW COOKER:
2- to 3 1/2-quart

PREP TIME:
20 minutes

COOK TIME:
Low 6 to 8 hours

Betty's Success Tip

Turkey sausage is lower in fat than pork sausage but still is high in flavor! Check the label on the sausage you select to be sure it is made with turkey breast, which is lower in fat than turkey sausage made with dark meat.

Ingredient Substitution

A *cassoulet* is a classic French dish of dried white beans and various meats. Traditionally, it is covered and cooked very slowly to blend the flavors, so making it in a slow cooker is ideal. This cassoulet takes a shortcut by using canned beans and turkey sausage. You can use any canned beans you have on hand, such as butter, kidney or black beans, and voilà— you'll still have a wonderful cassoulet.

1/2 pound fully cooked smoked turkey sausage ring, cut into 1/2-inch slices

1 medium carrot, shredded (2/3 cup)

1 small onion chopped (1/4 cup)

2 cans (15 or 16 ounces each) great northern beans, drained and 3/4 cup liquid reserved

1 teaspoon dried marjoram leaves

1/4 teaspoon dried thyme leaves

1/4 teaspoon pepper

1. Mix all ingredients including reserved bean liquid in 2- to 3 1/2-quart slow cooker.

2. Cover and cook on low heat setting 6 to 8 hours or until vegetables are tender.

1 Serving: Calories 340 (Calories from Fat 55); Fat 6g (Saturated 2g); Cholesterol 30mg; Sodium 580mg; Carbohydrate 57g (Dietary Fiber 14g); Protein 29g

% Daily Value: Vitamin A 24%; Vitamin C 2%; Calcium 20%; Iron 48%

Diet Exchanges: 3 Starch, 2 Very Lean Meat, 2 Vegetable

Pheasant in Mushroom Sauce

■ *8 servings* ■

SLOW COOKER:
3 1/2- to 6-quart

PREP TIME:
15 minutes

COOK TIME:
Low 6 to 7 hours

2 pheasants, cut into fourths

1/2 cup chicken broth

2 tablespoons all-purpose flour

1 tablespoon Worcestershire sauce

1 teaspoon salt

1 medium onion, chopped (1/2 cup)

1 clove garlic, finely chopped

1 can (10 3/4 ounces) condensed cream of chicken soup

1 can (4 ounces) sliced mushrooms, drained

Paprika

1. Place pheasant pieces in 3 1/2- to 6-quart slow cooker. Mix remaining ingredients except paprika; pour over pheasant. Sprinkle generously with paprika.

2. Cover and cook on low heat setting 6 to 7 hours or until pheasant is tender.

1 Serving: Calories 400 (Calories from Fat 180); Fat 20g (Saturated 6g); Cholesterol 130mg; Sodium 790mg; Carbohydrate 7g (Dietary Fiber 0g); Protein 46g

% Daily Value: Vitamin A 10%; Vitamin C 2%; Calcium 8%; Iron 50%

Diet Exchanges: 1/2 Starch, 7 Lean Meat

Ingredient Substitution

Have a little white wine left in the bottle? Use 1/2 cup wine instead of the chicken broth for an elegant little twist.

Serving Suggestion

Serve garlic mashed potatoes to enjoy with the creamy mushroom sauce. Add broccoli spears topped with a sprinkle of grated fresh lemon peel to round out the flavors.

Finishing Touch

You don't have to serve pheasant under glass to make it special. Mix together some crisply cooked and crumbled bacon, toasted chopped hazelnuts and chopped fresh parsley to sprinkle over each serving.

Wild Duck Breast à l'Orange

■ 4 servings ■

SLOW COOKER:
3 1/2- to 6-quart

PREP TIME:
20 minutes

COOK TIME:
Low 8 to 10 hours

Betty's Success Tip

The addition of the fresh oranges, apple and onion enhances the natural flavor of wild duck. However, these ingredients do pick up the wild flavor from the cooking juices of the duck. Most people find they don't care for the flavor of the fruit and onion after it is cooked, so we suggest discarding them.

Finishing Touch

The Pear-Orange Conserve on page 180 is an excellent accompaniment to the hearty flavor of wild duck breast. The conserve can be made three weeks ahead, and ready in the refrigerator.

2 whole wild duck breasts, cut in half and skin removed

1/2 teaspoon salt

1/4 teaspoon pepper

2 small oranges, peeled and cut into 1/2-inch pieces

1 medium apple, cut into 1/2-inch pieces

1 medium onion, cut into eighths

1 can (6 ounces) frozen orange juice concentrate, thawed

1. Sprinkle duck with salt and pepper. Layer duck, oranges, apple and onion in 3 1/2- to 6-quart slow cooker. Pour orange juice concentrate over top.

2. Cover and cook on low heat setting 8 to 10 hours or until duck is tender.

3. Remove duck from cooker. Discard fruit and onion mixture.

1 Serving: Calories 290 (Calories from Fat 110); Fat 12g (Saturated 4g); Cholesterol 110mg; Sodium 420mg; Carbohydrate 3g (Dietary Fiber 0g); Protein 42g

% Daily Value: Vitamin A 5%; Vitamin C 12%; Calcium 6%; Iron 60%

Diet Exchanges: 5 Very Lean Meat, 2 Fat

Meatless Main Dishes

◄ *Lentil and Mixed-Vegetable Casserole (page 154)*

Wild Rice with Cranberries

■ 4 servings ■

SLOW COOKER:
2- to 3 1/2-quart

PREP TIME:
15 minutes

COOK TIME:
Low 4 to 5 hours

FINISHING COOK TIME:
Low 15 minutes

Betty's Success Tip

Toasting the almonds not only enhances the flavor and color of the almonds but also helps prevent them from becoming soggy after they are stirred into the wild rice mixture.

Ingredient Substitution

Many supermarkets now carry a wide variety of dried fruits. Dried blueberries or cherries are a delicious substitute for the cranberries.

Serving Suggestion

Cooked broccoli spears are a tasty companion for wild rice and cranberries. Make an easy cheese sauce for the broccoli by melting some cubes of process cheese loaf in the microwave.

1 1/2 cups uncooked wild rice

1 tablespoon margarine or butter, melted

1/2 teaspoon salt

1/4 teaspoon pepper

4 medium green onions, sliced (1/4 cup)

2 cans (14 1/2 ounces each) ready-to-serve vegetable broth

1 can (4 ounces) sliced mushrooms, undrained

1/2 cup slivered almonds, toasted (page 152)

1/3 cup dried cranberries

1. Mix all ingredients except almonds and cranberries in 2- to 3 1/2-quart slow cooker.

2. Cover and cook on low heat setting 4 to 5 hours or until wild rice is tender.

3. Stir in almonds and cranberries.

4. Cover and cook on low heat setting 15 minutes.

1 Serving: Calories 150 (Calories from Fat 35); Fat 4g (Saturated 1g); Cholesterol 0mg; Sodium 560mg; Carbohydrate 26g (Dietary Fiber 2g); Protein 5g

% Daily Value: Vitamin A 2%; Vitamin C 2%; Calcium 4%; Iron 6%

Diet Exchanges: 1 Starch, 2 Vegetable, 1/2 Fat

Easy Baked Beans

■ 10 servings ■

Crowd
SIZE

SLOW COOKER:
3 1/2- to 6-quart

PREP TIME:
10 minutes

COOK TIME:
Low 4 to 5 hours
High 2 to 2 1/2 hours

2 cans (28 ounces each) vegetarian baked beans, drained

1 medium onion, chopped (1/2 cup)

2/3 cup barbecue sauce

1/2 cup packed brown sugar

2 tablespoons ground mustard (dry)

1. Mix all ingredients in 3 1/2- to 6-quart slow cooker.

2. Cover and cook on low heat setting 4 to 5 hours (or high heat setting 2 to 2 1/2 hours) or until desired consistency.

1 Serving: Calories 190 (Calories from Fat 10); Fat 1g (Saturated 0g); Cholesterol 0mg; Sodium 940mg; Carbohydrate 43g (Dietary Fiber 8g); Protein 10g

% Daily Value: Vitamin A 0%; Vitamin C 2%; Calcium 10%; Iron 18%

Diet Exchanges: 1 Starch, 2 Vegetable, 1 Fruit

Betty's Success Tip

This recipe is so quick and easy that you will want make it for just the family, too. Cut the ingredients in half, and cook in a 2- to 3 1/2-quart slow cooker.

Serving Suggestion

Spoon the beans over squares of hot corn bread or split corn bread muffins. Sprinkle with shredded Cheddar cheese and sliced green onion.

Finishing Touch

To keep this a meatless treat, sprinkle each serving with bacon-flavor bits. You'll love that great smoky flavor that goes so well with baked beans.

Old-Fashioned Baked Beans

■ *12 servings* ■

SLOW COOKER:
4- to 6-quart

PREP TIME:
10 minutes

COOK TIME:
High 2 hours

STAND TIME:
8 hours

FINISHING COOK TIME:
Low 10 to 12 hours

2 pounds dried navy beans (4 cups), sorted and rinsed

9 cups water

2/3 cup packed brown sugar

2/3 cup molasses

1 tablespoon mustard

1 teaspoon salt

1 large onion, chopped (1 cup)

1. Place beans and water in 4- to 6-quart slow cooker.

2. Cover and cook on high heat setting 2 hours. Turn off heat; let stand 8 hours to 24 hours.

3. Stir in remaining ingredients.

4. Cover and cook on low heat setting 10 to 12 hours or until beans are very tender and most of the liquid is absorbed.

1 Serving: Caiories 310 (Calories from Fat 10); Fat 1g (Saturated 0g); Cholesterol 0mg; Sodium 230mg; Carbohydrate 71g (Dietary Fiber 11g); Protein 15g

% Daily Value: Vitamin A 0%; Vitamin C 2%; Calcium 16%; Iron 30%

Diet Exchanges: 2 Starch, 2 Vegetable, 2 Fruit

Betty's Success Tip

Baked beans can be eaten as an entrée or served alongside a grilled veggie burger. To serve these beans as a side dish, you may want to cut the recipe in half and cook it in a 2- to 3 1/2-quart slow cooker.

Ingredient Substitution

Dried navy beans are probably the most popular bean for old-fashioned baked beans, but you can use other beans. Great Northern, lima and pinto beans all will work because they cook in the same length of time.

Finishing Touch

To create a rich autumn flavor, stir one or two peeled and chopped apples into the beans for the last 30 minutes of cooking.

Old-Fashioned Baked Beans ➤

Cuban Black Beans and Rice

▪ *6 servings* ▪

SLOW COOKER:
3 1/2- to 6-quart

PREP TIME:
20 minutes

COOK TIME:
High 6 to 8 hours

Serving Suggestion

Try serving these black beans with poached eggs instead of rice. Place a poached egg on top of each serving of beans. Spoon your favorite salsa or drizzle hot sauce onto the egg, and top it off with a sprinkle of shredded Cheddar cheese and chopped fresh cilantro.

Finishing Touch

Serve bowls of chopped red onion and hard-cooked eggs to sprinkle on top for a traditional black bean and rice dish.

1 pound dried black beans (2 cups), sorted and rinsed

1 large onion, chopped (1 cup)

1 large bell pepper, chopped (1 1/2 cups)

5 cloves garlic, finely chopped

2 bay leaves

1 can (14 1/2 ounces) diced tomatoes, undrained

5 cups water

2 tablespoons olive or vegetable oil

4 teaspoons ground cumin

2 teaspoons finely chopped jalapeño chili

1 teaspoon salt

3 cups hot cooked rice, for serving

1. Mix all ingredients except rice in 3 1/2- to 6-quart slow cooker.

2. Cover and cook on high heat setting 6 to 8 hours or until beans are tender and most of the liquid is absorbed. Remove bay leaves.

3. Serve beans over rice.

1 Serving: Calories 385 (Calories from Fat 55); Fat 6g (Saturated 1g); Cholesterol 0mg; Sodium 500mg; Carbohydrate 78g (Dietary Fiber 14g); Protein 19g

% Daily Value: Vitamin A 6%; Vitamin C 32%; Calcium 18%; Iron 38%

Diet Exchanges: 4 Starch, 3 Vegetable

White Beans with Sun-Dried Tomatoes

■ 5 servings ■

SLOW COOKER:
3 1/2- to 6-quart

PREP TIME:
10 minutes

COOK TIME:
High 4 to 5 hours

1 pound dried great Northern beans (2 cups), sorted and rinsed

2 cloves garlic, crushed

6 cups water

1 1/2 teaspoons dried basil leaves

1 teaspoon salt

1/4 teaspoon pepper

3/4 cup finely chopped sun-dried tomatoes in olive oil

1 can (2 1/4 ounces) sliced ripe olives, drained

1. Mix all ingredients except tomatoes and olives in 3 1/2- to 6-quart slow cooker.

2. Cover and cook on high heat setting 4 to 5 hours or until beans are tender.

3. Stir in tomatoes and olives.

Ingredient Substitution

Sun-dried tomatoes add a robust meaty flavor and a bit of chewiness to this dish. You can add a cup of finely chopped seeded fresh tomatoes instead of the sun-dried tomatoes if you want.

Serving Suggestion

Serve with a large crisp tossed green salad dressed with an olive oil-balsamic vinaigrette, along with slices of French baguette. A glass of red wine makes this a perfect meal.

1 Serving: Calories 300 (Calories from Fat 35); Fat 4g (Saturated 1g); Cholesterol 0mg; Sodium 640mg; Carbohydrate 62g (Dietary Fiber 16g); Protein 23g

% Daily Value: Vitamin A 2%; Vitamin C 14%; Calcium 22%; Iron 52%

Diet Exchanges: 3 Starch, 3 Vegetable

Savory Garbanzo Beans with Vegetables

■ *8 servings* ■

SLOW COOKER:
3 1/2- to 6-quart

PREP TIME:
15 minutes

COOK TIME:
High 4 to 5 hours

FINISHING COOK TIME:
High 15 minutes

Betty's Success Tip

Sautéing the vegetables in olive oil before stirring them into the cooked beans not only enhances the flavor but also helps to reduce some of the liquid from the fresh mushrooms.

Ingredient Substitution

A drained 8-ounce can of sliced mushrooms can be used instead of the fresh mushrooms. You can skip the sautéing in step 3 and just add the canned mushrooms, carrots, onions and garlic to the cooked beans. Stir in a tablespoon of olive oil for added flavor.

Finishing Touch

Enhance the flavor with an additional squeeze of fresh lemon juice and a dash of lemon pepper seasoning before serving.

1 pound dried garbanzo beans (2 cups), sorted and rinsed

5 1/2 cups water

1 teaspoon salt

1/2 teaspoon pepper

2 tablespoons olive or vegetable oil

2 cups sliced mushrooms

1 cup shredded carrots (1 1/2 medium)

4 medium green onions, thinly sliced (1/4 cup)

2 cloves garlic, finely chopped

2 tablespoons lemon juice

1 to 2 tablespoons prepared horseradish

2 teaspoons mustard

1. Place beans, water, salt and pepper in 3 1/2- to 6-quart slow cooker.

2. Cover and cook on high heat setting 4 to 5 hours or until beans are tender.

3. Heat oil in 12-inch skillet over medium heat. Cook mushrooms, carrots, onions, and garlic in oil about 5 minutes, stirring occasionally, until vegetables are tender. Stir vegetables into beans. Stir in remaining ingredients.

4. Cover and cook on high heat setting 15 minutes to blend flavors.

1 Serving: Calories 210 (Calories from Fat 65); Fat 7g (Saturated 1g); Cholesterol 0mg; Sodium 330mg; Carbohydrate 36g (Dietary Fiber 10g); Protein 11g

% Daily Value: Vitamin A 24%; Vitamin C 4%; Calcium 6%; Iron 22%

Diet Exchanges: 2 Starch, 1 Vegetable, 1 Fat

Red Beans and Rice

▪ *8 servings* ▪

SLOW COOKER:
3 1/2- to 6-quart

PREP TIME:
20 minutes

COOK TIME:
High 4 to 5 hours

FINISHING COOK TIME:
High 15 to 20 minutes

Betty's Success Tip

We found we had good results using instant rice in recipes in the slow cooker. Instant rice is fully or partially cooked before it is dehydrated and packaged. It produces less starch, so the finished dish is not sticky like some dishes that use regular long-grain rice.

Serving Suggestion

It has been said that red beans and rice were a favorite Monday evening supper in the New Orleans area. Monday was spent doing the laundry while the red beans were left to simmer on the stove. Today, the red beans can be left to simmer in the slow cooker while you are busy doing other things. Serve with corn bread or hot baking powder biscuits.

Finishing Touch

Avocado and rice are a natural together. For a taste sensation, squeeze the juice of half a large lime over a couple of chopped large avocados, and gently toss to blend the flavors. Spoon over the top of the rice and beans, and sprinkle with sliced green onion.

1 pound dried kidney beans (2 cups), sorted and rinsed

1 large green bell pepper, chopped (1 1/2 cups)

1 large onion, chopped (1 cup)

2 cloves garlic, finely chopped

7 cups water

1 1/2 teaspoons salt

1/4 teaspoon pepper

2 cups uncooked instant rice

Red pepper sauce

1. Mix all ingredients except rice and pepper sauce in 3 1/2- to 6-quart slow cooker.

2. Cover and cook on high heat setting 4 to 5 hours or until beans are tender.

3. Stir in rice.

4. Cover and cook on high heat setting 15 to 20 minutes or until rice is tender. Serve with pepper sauce.

1 Serving: Calories 250 (Calories from Fat 10); Fat 1g (Saturated 0g); Cholesterol 0mg; Sodium 460mg; Carbohydrate 57g (Dietary Fiber 10g); Protein 14g

% Daily Value: Vitamin A 0%; Vitamin C 18%; Calcium 4%; Iron 28%

Diet Exchanges: 3 Starch, 2 Vegetable

Tex-Mex Pinto Beans

■ 6 servings ■

SLOW COOKER:
3 1/2- to 6-quart

PREP TIME:
10 minutes

COOK TIME:
High 7 to 9 hours

1 pound dried pinto beans (2 cups), sorted and rinsed

1 large onion, chopped (1 cup)

2 cloves garlic, finely chopped

6 1/2 cups water

1 tablespoon chili powder

1 1/2 teaspoons salt

1/2 teaspoon pepper

1. Mix all ingredients in 3 1/2- to 6-quart slow cooker.

2. Cover and cook on high heat setting 7 to 9 hours or until beans are tender.

1 Serving: Calories 200 (Calories from Fat 10); Fat 1g (Saturated 0g); Cholesterol 0mg; Sodium 610mg; Carbohydrate 49g (Dietary Fiber 16g); Protein 15g

% Daily Value: Vitamin A 4%; Vitamin C 4%; Calcium 10%; Iron 26%

Diet Exchanges: 2 Starch, 4 Vegetable

Ingredient Substitution

To make this easy recipe even easier, use 1/4 teaspoon garlic powder or 1/2 teaspoon chopped garlic from a jar to save a few minutes.

Serving Suggestion

Nothing complements beans like hot corn bread slathered with butter. Add a big bowl of your favorite creamy cabbage salad and tall glasses of lemonade for a "Southern moment" at your supper table.

Finishing Touch

If you like more punch to your Tex-Mex dishes, pass the bottle of hot red pepper sauce or some crushed red pepper at the table, so everyone can have just the right seasoning.

Spicy Black-Eyed Peas

■ *8 servings* ■

SLOW COOKER:
3 1/2- to 6-quart

PREP TIME:
5 minutes

COOK TIME:
High 3 to 4 hours

FINISHING COOK TIME:
High 10 minutes

1 pound dried black-eyed peas (2 cups), sorted and rinsed

1 medium onion, chopped (1/2 cup)

6 cups water

1 teaspoon salt

1/2 teaspoon pepper

3/4 cup medium or hot salsa

1. Mix all ingredients except salsa in 3 1/2- to 6-quart slow cooker.

2. Cover and cook on high heat setting 3 to 4 hours or until peas are tender.

3. Stir in salsa.

4. Cover and cook on high heat setting about 10 minutes or until hot.

1 Serving: Calories 145 (Calories from Fat 10); Fat 1g (Saturated 0g); Cholesterol 0mg; Sodium 360mg; Carbohydrate 35g (Dietary Fiber 11g); Protein 13g

% Daily Value: Vitamin A 2%; Vitamin C 4%; Calcium 4%; Iron 22%

Diet Exchanges: 1 Starch, 4 Vegetable

Betty's Success Tip

We like the extra flavor of hot salsa that goes so well with black-eyed peas, but you use whichever salsa suits your family's taste—mild, medium or hot.

Serving Suggestion

Cooked greens, such as spinach, mustard or collards, are the perfect mate for black-eyed peas. Serve the greens with red wine vinegar to splash on top. Warm cornbread with molasses completes the meal.

Finishing Touch

For an extra-special touch, top each serving with sour cream and a big spoonful of salsa. You can use purchased salsa, but your home-made chunky salsa adds a nice texture contrast to the cooked peas.

Barbecued Limas

6 servings

SLOW COOKER:
3 1/2- to 6-quart

PREP TIME:
10 minutes

COOK TIME:
Low 7 to 8 hours

Betty's Success Tip

We found that canned beans taste and look better when cooked on low rather than on the high setting because the beans won't overcook and become mushy. The long, slow cooking enhances the already-cooked beans with the flavors of the other ingredients in this dish.

Ingredient Substitution

Maple syrup adds a sweetness that complements the delicate flavor of lima beans. You can use the same amount of molasses if you prefer a heartier flavor to go with the barbecue sauce. And if you want a bit of meat added to the beans, add a 1/2 cup chopped fully cooked ham.

Finishing Touch

For an extra taste treat, top these beans with additional barbecue sauce and sprinkle with bacon-flavor bits before serving.

2 bags (16 ounces each) frozen lima beans, thawed and drained

1 medium onion, chopped (1/2 cup)

2/3 cup vegetable broth

1/3 cup maple-flavored syrup

1/3 cup barbecue sauce

1/2 teaspoon salt

1/8 teaspoon pepper

1. Mix all ingredients in 3 1/2- to 6-quart slow cooker.

2. Cover and cook on low heat setting 7 to 8 hours or until beans are tender.

1 Serving: Calories 195 (Calories from Fat 10); Fat 1g (Saturated 0g); Cholesterol 0mg; Sodium 530mg; Carbohydrate 47g (Dietary Fiber 10g); Protein 10g

% Daily Value: Vitamin A 6%; Vitamin C 18%; Calcium 4%; Iron 12%

Diet Exchanges: 1 Starch, 3 Vegetable, 1 Fruit

Barley-Pine Nut Casserole

■ *5 servings* ■

SLOW COOKER: 3 1/2- to 6-quart	1 cup uncooked pearl barley
PREP TIME: 15 minutes	1 1/2 cups eight-vegetable juice
COOK TIME: Low 6 to 8 hours	1/2 teaspoon salt

1 cup uncooked pearl barley

1 1/2 cups eight-vegetable juice

1/2 teaspoon salt

1/4 teaspoon pepper

2 medium stalks celery, sliced (1 cup)

1 medium bell pepper, chopped (1 cup)

1 medium onion, chopped (1/2 cup)

1 can (14 1/2 ounces) ready-to-serve vegetable broth

4 medium green onions, sliced (1/4 cup)

1/4 cup pine nuts, toasted*

1. Mix all ingredients except green onions and nuts in 3 1/2- to 6-quart slow cooker.

2. Cover and cook on low heat setting 6 to 8 hours or until barley is tender.

3. Stir in green onions and nuts.

1 Serving: Calories 190 (Calories from Fat 35); Fat 4g (Saturated 1g); Cholesterol 0mg; Sodium 800mg; Carbohydrate 41g (Dietary Fiber 9g); Protein 6g

% Daily Value: Vitamin A 16%; Vitamin C 38%; Calcium 4%; Iron 10%

Diet Exchanges: 2 Starch, 2 Vegetable

To toast nuts, bake uncovered in ungreased shallow pan in 350° oven about 10 minutes, stirring occasionally, until golden brown. Or cook in ungreased heavy skillet over medium-low heat 5 to 7 minutes, stirring frequently until browning begins, then stirring constantly until golden brown.

Betty's Success Tip

Pearl barley, which is the most common form, is the perfect grain to cook in the slow cooker. The long, slow cooking produces barley that is tender but not gummy.

Ingredient Substitution

Pine nuts, or piñons, are the sweet edible seeds of pine trees that grow in the southwestern United States and in Mexico. Toasted, they add an interesting nutty flavor and texture to the casserole, but almonds can be substituted. Try the spicy eight-vegetable juice for a more robust flavor.

Serving Suggestion

Although this can be a hearty meatless meal for anyone, this also makes the perfect side dish to serve with beef, lamb, pork or chicken.

Lentil and Mixed-Vegetable Casserole

■ 8 servings ■

SLOW COOKER
3 1/2- to 6-quart

PREP TIME:
5 minutes

COOK TIME:
Low 2 to 2¹/₂ hours

FINISHING COOK TIME:
Low 30 minutes

1 pound dried lentils (2 cups), sorted and rinsed

2 cans (14 1/2 ounces each) ready-to-serve vegetable broth

1/2 teaspoon salt

1/4 teaspoon pepper

1 bag (16 ounces) frozen broccoli, cauliflower and carrots, thawed and drained

1 can (10 3/4 ounces) condensed golden mushroom soup

1. Mix lentils, broth, salt and pepper in 3 1/2- to 6-quart slow cooker.

2. Cover and cook on low heat setting 2 to 2 1/2 hours or until lentils are tender.

3. Stir in vegetables and soup.

4. Cover and cook on low heat setting about 30 minutes or until vegetable are tender.

1 Serving: Calories 185 (Calories from Fat 25); Fat 3g (Saturated 1g); Cholesterol 0mg; Sodium 880mg; Carbohydrate 38g (Dietary Fiber 14g); Protein 16g

% Daily Value: Vitamin A 26%; Vitamin C 18%; Calcium 6%; Iron 32%

Diet Exchanges: 1 Starch, 4 Vegetable

Betty's Success Tip

Lentils are carefully cleaned before they are packaged, but poorer-quality lentils sometimes do slip by. Carefully sort through the lentils and remove any that are too light or dark. It is good to rinse the lentils in water before cooking to be sure they are clean.

Ingredient Substitution

We like the flavors and colors of the broccoli, cauliflower and carrots, but feel free to use any vegetable blend that you like and be creative with this casserole. The same goes for the flavor of the soup—cream of mushroom or cream of broccoli also would make a tasty dish.

Finishing Touch

Sprinkle a cup of shredded mozzarella cheese over the top of the casserole before serving. The heat of the dish will soften the cheese. Sliced process American cheese, cut into strips, or shredded process cheese loaf also works nicely because the cheese will melt on top of the hot dish.

Mediterranean Bulgur and Lentils

8 servings

SLOW COOKER:
3 1/2- to 6-quart

PREP TIME:
15 minutes

COOK TIME:
Low 3 to 4 hours

FINISHING COOK TIME:
High 15 minutes

Ingredient Substitution

If you are out of ground cumin, use the same amount of chili powder. And instead of chopping fresh garlic, you can use 1/4 teaspoon garlic powder.

Serving Suggestion

You have a little of everything in one dish—grains, vegetables and cheese. A green salad made of tender Bibb lettuce is a nice addition. Serve with olive oil to drizzle on the greens and lemon wedges to squeeze fresh juice over the top. Use warm pita bread wedges to scoop up every bit of this dish.

Finishing Touch

Before sprinkling the feta over this dish, stir together an 8-ounce container of plain yogurt and 1 1/2 teaspoons dried mint leaves or 1 tablespoon chopped fresh mint leaves. Spoon over the dish, then top with the feta. You'll love the refreshing mint flavor with this Mediterranean-inspired dish.

1 cup uncooked bulgur or cracked wheat

1/2 cup dried lentils, sorted and rinsed

1 teaspoon ground cumin

1/4 teaspoon salt

3 cloves garlic, finely chopped

1 can (15 1/4 ounces) whole kernel corn, drained

2 cans (14 1/2 ounces each) ready-to-serve vegetable broth

2 medium tomatoes, chopped (1 1/2 cups)

1 can (2 1/4 ounces) sliced ripe olives, drained

1 cup crumbled feta cheese

1. Mix all ingredients except tomatoes, olives and cheese in 3 1/2- to 6-quart slow cooker.

2. Cover and cook on low heat setting 3 to 4 hours or until lentils are tender.

3. Stir in tomatoes and olives.

4. Cover and cook on high heat setting 15 minutes.

5. Top with cheese.

1 Serving: Calories 200 (Calories from Fat 55); Fat 6g (Saturated 3g); Cholesterol 15mg; Sodium 920mg; Carbohydrate 34g (Dietary Fiber 8g); Protein 10g

% Daily Value: Vitamin A 12%; Vitamin C 10%; Calcium 12%; Iron 14%

Diet Exchanges: 2 Starch, 1 Vegetable, 1/2 Fat

Bulgur Pilaf with Broccoli and Carrots

■ 8 servings ■

SLOW COOKER:
3 1/2- to 6-quart

PREP TIME:
20 minutes

COOK TIME:
Low 6 to 8 hours

FINISHING COOK TIME:
High 15 minutes

2 cups uncooked bulgur or cracked wheat

1 tablespoon margarine or butter, melted

1 teaspoon salt

4 medium carrots, shredded (2 2/3 cups)

1 large onion, chopped (1 cup)

2 cans (14 1/2 ounces each) ready-to-serve vegetable broth

4 cups chopped fresh broccoli

1 cup shredded Colby cheese (4 ounces)

1. Mix all ingredients except broccoli and cheese in 3 1/2- to 6-quart slow cooker.

2. Cover and cook on low setting 6 to 8 hours or just until bulgur is tender.

3. Stir in broccoli. Sprinkle with cheese. Cover and cook on high setting about 15 minutes or until broccoli is tender and cheese is melted.

1 Serving: Calories 205 (Calories from Fat 65); Fat 7g (Saturated 3g); Cholesterol 15mg; Sodium 880mg; Carbohydrate 35g (Dietary Fiber 9g); Protein 10g

% Daily Value: Vitamin A 64%; Vitamin C 38%; Calcium 12%; Iron 8%

Diet Exchanges: 2 Starch, 1 Vegetable, 1 Fat

Betty's Success Tip

Chop the broccoli stems and flow-erets into about 1/2-inch pieces, so they will be tender but still a little crisp when cooked to add a pleasant crunch. Or use 4 cups of thawed frozen chopped broccoli to save some time. Cut any large pieces of broccoli into smaller pieces, so they all will cook in the same amount of time.

Ingredient Substitution

Using cauliflower instead of broc-coli will not be as colorful but will be just as tasty with the carrots and cheese. A light sprinkling of ground nutmeg over the melted cheese will add a delicate spicy flavor and a bit of color.

Serving Suggestion

A nice change of pace from the more common rice pilaf, this meatless bulgur entrée is sure to satisfy both young and old. Serve with a fresh citrus fruit salad of orange and grapefruit sections. Drizzle with a poppy seed fruit dressing or your favorite fruit salad dressing.

Bulgur Pilaf with Broccoli and Carrots ➤

Three-Grain Medley

■ *6 servings* ■

SLOW COOKER:
3 1/2- to 6-quart

PREP TIME:
10 minutes

COOK TIME:
Low 4 to 6 hours

Betty's Success Tip

Wheat berries, barley and wild rice merge for a tasty mix of textures in this main-dish entrée. Because all three grains take the same amount of time to cook, they all will be tender and not overcooked. If you want to mix different grains, be sure to select those that require the same amount of cooking time. If you can't find wheat berries at your local market, check out any natural foods store.

Ingredient Substitution

Instead of the pimientos, soak sun-dried tomatoes in water until tender, then chop them and add to this grain mixture. Use about 1/4 cup of the chopped tomatoes.

Serving Suggestion

Use this scrumptious grain filling to stuff bell pepper shells. Steam cleaned bell pepper halves (any color that you are in the mood for) just until tender so that they still hold their shape. Spoon the hot cooked grain mixture into the halves, and sprinkle with shredded Parmesan cheese.

2/3 cup uncooked wheat berries

1/2 cup uncooked pearl barley

1/2 cup uncooked wild rice

1/4 cup chopped fresh parsley

1/4 cup margarine or butter, melted

2 teaspoons finely shredded lemon peel

6 medium green onions, thinly sliced (6 tablespoons)

2 cloves garlic, finely chopped

2 cans (14 1/2 ounces each) ready-to-serve vegetable broth

1 jar (2 ounces) diced pimientos, undrained

1. Mix all ingredients in 3 1/2- to 6-quart slow cooker.

2. Cover and cook on low heat setting 4 to 6 hours or until liquid is absorbed. Stir before serving.

1 Serving: Calories 230 (Calories from Fat 70); Fat 8g (Saturated 0g); Cholesterol 0mg; Sodium 710mg; Carbohydrate 40g (Dietary Fiber 7g); Protein 6g

% Daily Value: Vitamin A 24%; Vitamin C 12%; Calcium 4%; Iron 10%

Diet Exchanges: 2 Starch, 2 Vegetable, 1/2 Fat

Marinara Sauce with Spaghetti

■ 12 servings ■

SLOW COOKER:
3 1/2- to 6-quart

PREP TIME:
15 minutes

COOK TIME:
Low 8 to 10 hours
High 4 to 5 hours

Betty's Success Tip

This multipurpose sauce is so easy to make that you'll want to make it often and keep a few extra containers in the freezer. Ladle the cooked sauce into airtight freezer containers, and keep in your freezer up to a month. Just thaw in the refrigerator or microwave, and use in your favorite recipe.

Ingredient Substitution

The crushed tomatoes with Italian herbs add extra flavor, but you can use plain crushed tomatoes and increase the basil to 1 tablespoon and the oregano to 2 teaspoons.

Serving Suggestion

Make primavera sauce for your family by cutting the recipe in half and stirring in 2 cups of mixed cooked vegetables, such as broccoli, cauliflower, sliced carrots, mushrooms and peas, after step 2. Cover and cook until the vegetables are hot, which will take about 15 minutes on high. Serve over your favorite cooked pasta, and sprinkle with shredded Parmesan cheese.

2 cans (28 ounces each) crushed tomatoes with Italian herbs, undrained

1 can (6 ounces) tomato paste

1 large onion, chopped (1 cup)

8 cloves garlic, finely chopped

1 tablespoon olive or vegetable oil

2 teaspoons sugar

2 teaspoons dried basil leaves

1 teaspoon dried oregano leaves

1 teaspoon salt

1 teaspoon pepper

12 cups hot cooked spaghetti, for serving

Shredded Parmesan cheese, if desired

1. Mix all ingredients except spaghetti and cheese in 3 1/2- to 6-quart slow cooker.

2. Cover and cook on low heat setting 8 to 10 hours (or high heat setting 4 to 5 hours).

3. Serve sauce over spaghetti. Sprinkle with cheese.

1 Serving: Calories 255 (Calories from Fat 20); Fat 2g (Saturated 0g); Cholesterol 0mg; Sodium 670mg; Carbohydrate 54g (Dietary Fiber 4g); Protein 9g

% Daily Value: Vitamin A 8%; Vitamin C 18%; Calcium 6%; Iron 16%

Diet Exchanges: 3 Starch, 2 Vegetable

Great Serve Withs

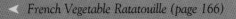

◄ *French Vegetable Ratatouille (page 166)*

Red Cabbage with Apples

■ *8 servings* ■

SLOW COOKER:
3 1/2- to 6-quart

PREP TIME:
15 minutes

COOK TIME:
Low 6 to 8 hours

1 medium head red cabbage, coarsely shredded (8 cups)

2 medium tart red apples, sliced

2 tablespoons sugar

3 tablespoons water

3 tablespoons cider vinegar

1 tablespoon margarine or butter, melted

1 teaspoon salt

1/4 teaspoon pepper

1. Mix all ingredients in 3 1/2- to 6-quart slow cooker.

2. Cover and cook on low heat setting 6 to 8 hours or until cabbage is very tender.

1 Serving: Calories 70 (Calories from Fat 20); Fat 2g (Saturated 0g); Cholesterol 0mg; Sodium 330mg; Carbohydrate 14g (Dietary Fiber 3g); Protein 2g

% Daily Value: Vitamin A 4%; Vitamin C 30%; Calcium 4%; Iron 4%

Diet Exchanges: 2 Vegetable, 1/2 Fruit

Betty's Success Tip

Shredding cabbage is easy if you use a long, sharp knife. Remove the tough outer leaves from the cabbage head. Cut the cabbage, through the core, into fourths. Remove the core, and cut the cabbage across the leaves into thin slices. The leaves will separate into long, thin pieces of cabbage. If you have a food processor with the slicing attachment, the work is even easier!

Ingredient Substitution

Apples with red cabbage is a popular combination, but you may want to add a cup of chopped dried apricots or pears instead of the apples for a different twist.

Serving Suggestion

The sweet and sour flavors of this cabbage dish go nicely with pork chops or roast pork or duck. If you are a fan of wild duck, this is the perfect side dish to complement its hearty flavor.

Scalloped Corn

■ 8 servings ■

SLOW COOKER:
2- to 4-quart

PREP TIME:
15 minutes

COOK TIME:
High 2 to 3 hours

Ingredient Substitution

If you like onion, add a chopped small onion with the whole kernel corn. For a little more kick, also stir in a drained 4-ounce can of chopped green chilies.

Serving Suggestion

Have a good-ole-Southern supper on the back porch. Serve maple syrup to drizzle over this scalloped corn, thick slices of baked ham right off the grill and your favorite potato salad. A tall pitcher of icy tea garnished with fresh mint leaves completes the setting.

Finishing Touch

Sprinkling crushed crackers or corn chips over the top of the scalloped corn before serving adds a nice touch of crunch. Or for a Mexican corn dish, sprinkle about a cup of shredded process cheese spread loaf with jalapeño peppers over the top before serving.

2/3 cup all-purpose flour

1/4 cup margarine or butter, melted

1 cup fat-free cholesterol-free egg product

3/4 cup evaporated milk

2 teaspoons sugar

1 teaspoon salt

1/8 teaspoon pepper

1 can (14 3/4 ounces) cream-style corn

1 can (15 1/4 ounces) whole kernel corn, drained

1. Spray inside of 2- to 4-quart slow cooker with cooking spray.

2. Mix all ingredients except whole kernel corn in large bowl until well mixed. Stir in whole kernel corn; pour into cooker.

3. Cover and cook on high heat setting 2 to 3 hours or until set.

1 Serving: Calories 220 (Calories from Fat 70); Fat 8g (Saturated 2g); Cholesterol 5mg; Sodium 670mg; Carbohydrate 32g (Dietary Fiber 3g); Protein 8g

% Daily Value: Vitamin A 12%; Vitamin C 8%; Calcium 8%; Iron 10%

Diet Exchanges: 2 Starch, 1/2 Fat

Ginger Squash

■ 4 servings ■

SLOW COOKER:
5- to 6-quart

PREP TIME:
15 minutes

COOK TIME:
High 3 to 4 hours

2 small acorn squash (3/4 pound each)

1/4 cup water

1/4 cup packed brown sugar

1/4 cup margarine or butter, melted

3 tablespoons dry sherry or apple juice

1 1/2 teaspoons ground ginger

1/4 teaspoon salt

1. Cut squash crosswise in half; remove seeds and membranes

2. Pour water into 5- to 6-quart slow cooker. Place squash halves, cut sides up, in cooker. (It may be necessary to stack squash halves in cooker so they fit, but they still will cook evenly.)

3. Mix remaining ingredients; spoon into squash.

4. Cover and cook on high heat setting 3 to 4 hours or until squash are tender.

1 Serving: Calories 270 (Calories from Fat 110); Fat 12g (Saturated 2g); Cholesterol 0mg; Sodium 320mg; Carbohydrate 47g (Dietary Fiber 10g); Protein 3g

% Daily Value: Vitamin A 24%; Vitamin C 18%; Calcium 10%; Iron 12%

Diet Exchanges: 1 Starch, 2 Fruit, 2 Fat

Betty's Success Tip

Hard-skin squash such as acorn are not easy to cut before cooking. Here is a tip to make cutting squash easy: Pierce each squash with a knife several times. Microwave on High 3 to 4 minutes or just until squash is warm and skin starts to soften.

Ingredient Substitution

Cinnamon might have more family appeal, so use ground cinnamon instead of the ginger.

Finishing Touch

Fill the squash with chopped crisp, red apples and coarsely chopped toasted walnuts. Just add them to the sauce in the centers of the squash halves. Sprinkle chopped crystallized ginger around the edges of the squash for added flavor.

French Vegetable Ratatouille

■ 8 servings ■

SLOW COOKER:
3 1/2- to 6-quart

PREP TIME:
20 minutes

COOK TIME:
Low 6 to 8 hours

Ingredient Substitution

If you are a little short on time, a tablespoon of dried parsley flakes can be used instead of the fresh parsley, and 1/4 teaspoon of garlic powder can be used for the garlic cloves.

Serving Suggestion

This vegetable medley, known as *ratatouille*, has long been a favorite in southern France, especially during the summer harvest season. Create a one-dish meal by serving ragout over cooked pasta. Sprinkle with grated Romano cheese, and accompany with French bread.

1 small eggplant (1 pound), peeled and cut into 1/2-inch cubes (about 5 cups)

4 medium tomatoes, cut into fourths

1 medium zucchini, sliced

1 medium green bell pepper, cut into strips

1 medium onion, sliced

2 cloves garlic, finely chopped

1/4 cup chopped fresh parsley

2 tablespoons olive or vegetable oil

1 teaspoon salt

1 teaspoon dried basil leaves

1/4 teaspoon pepper

1. Mix all ingredients in 3 1/2- to 6-quart slow cooker.

2. Cover and cook on low heat setting 6 to 8 hours or until vegetables are tender.

1 Serving: Calories 70 (Calories from Fat 35); Fat 4g (Saturated 1g); Cholesterol 0mg; Sodium 300mg; Carbohydrate 10g (Dietary Fiber 3g); Protein 2g

% Daily Value: Vitamin A 6%; Vitamin C 26%; Calcium 2%; Iron 4%

Diet Exchanges: 2 Vegetable, 1/2 Fat

Scalloped Potatoes

■ 8 servings ■

SLOW COOKER:
3 1/2- to 6-quart

PREP TIME:
20 minutes

COOK TIME:
Low 10 to 12 hours

Ingredient Substitution

Vary the taste by using whatever cream soup you have on hand, such as cream of mushroom, chicken or broccoli. You may want to add a thinly sliced small onion or 1/4 teaspoon onion powder if you decide not to use the onion soup.

Finishing Touch

For the cheese lovers in your family, sprinkle about 1/2 cup of their favorite shredded cheese over the top of the potatoes. Cover and let stand a few minutes so the cheese becomes warm and melty.

6 medium potatoes (2 pounds), cut into 1/8-inch slices

1 can (10 3/4 ounces) condensed cream of onion soup

1 can (5 ounces) evaporated milk (2/3 cup)

1 jar (2 ounces) diced pimientos, undrained

1/2 teaspoon salt

1/4 teaspoon pepper

1. Spray inside of 3 1/2- to 6-quart slow cooker with cooking spray.

2. Mix all ingredients; pour into cooker.

3. Cover and cook on low heat setting 10 to 12 hours or until potatoes are tender.

1 Serving: Calories 155 (Calories from Fat 25); Fat 3g (Saturated 1g); Cholesterol 10mg; Sodium 460mg; Carbohydrate 30g (Dietary Fiber 2g); Protein 4g

% Daily Value: Vitamin A 4%; Vitamin C 16%; Calcium 10%; Iron 8%

Diet Exchanges: 2 Starch

Hot German Potato Salad

■ 6 servings ■

SLOW COOKER:
3 1/2- to 6-quart

PREP TIME:
15 minutes

COOK TIME:
Low 8 to 10 hours

Betty's Success Tip

We like to leave the skins on the potatoes because they are nutritious and add an interesting color to this hot salad. But you can peel the potatoes if you like.

Serving Suggestion

Create a simple German meal by serving this salad with grilled bratwurst or Polish sausage in buns. Crocks of dilled pickles or pickled beets and jars of mustard will add the final touch. To keep it simple, finish off the meal with crisp, juicy apples for dessert.

Finishing Touch

Add a touch of color and freshness by stirring in 3 tablespoons chopped fresh parsley with the bacon.

5 medium potatoes (about 1 3/4 pounds), cut into 1/4-inch slices

1 large onion, chopped (1 cup)

1/3 cup water

1/3 cup cider vinegar

2 tablespoons all-purpose flour

2 tablespoons sugar

1 teaspoon salt

1/2 teaspoon celery seed

1/4 teaspoon pepper

4 slices crisply cooked bacon, crumbled

1. Mix potatoes and onion in 3 1/2- to 6-quart slow cooker. Mix remaining ingredients except bacon; pour into cooker.

2. Cover and cook on low heat setting 8 to 10 hours or until potatoes are tender.

3. Stir in bacon.

1 Serving: Calories 160 (Calories from Fat 20); Fat 2g (Saturated 1g); Cholesterol 5mg; Sodium 470mg; Carbohydrate 35g (Dietary Fiber 3g); Protein 4g

% Daily Value: Vitamin A 0%; Vitamin C 12%; Calcium 2%; Iron 10%

Diet Exchanges: 2 Starch, 1 Vegetable

Sweet Potatoes with Applesauce

■ *6 servings* ■

SLOW COOKER:
2- to 3 1/2-quart

PREP TIME:
15 minutes

COOK TIME:
Low 6 to 8 hours

6 medium sweet potatoes or yams (2 pounds), peeled and cut into 1/2-inch cubes

1 1/2 cups applesauce

2/3 cup packed brown sugar

3 tablespoons margarine or butter, melted

1 teaspoon ground cinnamon

1/2 cup chopped nuts, toasted (page 152)

1. Place sweet potatoes in 2- to 3 1/2-quart slow cooker. Mix remaining ingredients except nuts; spoon over potatoes.

2. Cover and cook on low heat setting 6 to 8 hours or until potatoes are very tender.

3. Sprinkle with nuts.

1 Serving: Calories 350 (Calories from Fat 115); Fat 13g (Saturated 2g); Cholesterol 0mg; Sodium 100mg; Carbohydrate 60g (Dietary Fiber 5g); Protein 3g

% Daily Value: Vitamin A 100%; Vitamin C 24%; Calcium 6%; Iron 8%

Diet Exchanges: 2 Starch, 2 Fruit, 2 Fat

Betty's Success Tip

Many varieties of sweet potatoes are available, but a true yam is not available in our supermarkets. The variety of sweet potatoes with dark orange skin is often labeled as "yams." The very light-colored sweet potatoes are not as sweet and are drier than the darker-skin ones. We like the darker-skin sweet potatoes (or "yams") for this dish because they not only make a richer colored dish but also a tastier, sweeter one.

Serving Suggestion

While the turkey roasts in the oven, cook this Thanksgiving favorite in the cooker. If your home is this year's holiday gathering spot for family and friends, you can double or triple this recipe and cook it in a 5- to 6-quart cooker. And it will stay warm for second helpings.

Creamy Wild Rice

■ *10 servings* ■

SLOW COOKER:
5- to 6-quart

PREP TIME:
15 minutes

COOK TIME:
Low 8 to 9 hours

Betty's Success Tip

Wash wild rice in water before cooking it. Place the rice in a bowl of cold water and swirl it around with your hand. When the water becomes cloudy, drain the rice. Repeat the process until the water remains clear.

Serving Suggestion

Do you have a chicken or turkey roasting in the oven? The flavors of this wild rice dish go perfectly with them and can be made in the cooker, so you don't have to crowd the oven. Open a can of cranberry sauce, cook some green beans in the microwave, mash some potatoes and dinner will be ready in no time.

Finishing Touch

Toast some chopped nuts, such as walnuts or pecans, to add crunch and flavor to this creamy dish. Half a cup of nuts, either stirred in or sprinkled on top, should do the trick.

1 1/2 cups uncooked wild rice

2 1/4 cups water

1/2 teaspoon rubbed sage

1/2 teaspoon salt

1/4 teaspoon pepper

1 medium onion, chopped (1/2 cup)

1 can (10 3/4 ounces) condensed cream of celery soup

1 can (10 3/4 ounces) condensed cream of mushroom soup

1/4 cup chopped fresh parsley

1. Mix all ingredients except parsley in 5- to 6-quart slow cooker.

2. Cover and cook on low heat setting 8 to 9 hours or until wild rice is tender. Stir in parsley.

1 Serving: Calories 405 (Calories from Fat 115); Fat 13g (Saturated 2g); Cholesterol omg; Sodium 1360mg; Carbohydrate 69g (Dietary Fiber 11g); Protein 14g

% Daily Value: Vitamin A 18%; Vitamin C 10%; Calcium 6%; Iron 16%

Diet Exchanges: 2 Starch, 2 Vegetable, 2 Fruit, 2 Fat

Pecan Bread Stuffing

8 servings

SLOW COOKER:
2- to 3 1/2-quart

PREP TIME:
20 minutes

COOK TIME:
Low 4 to 5 hours

Betty's Success Tip

Making soft bread crumbs is easy because you just tear the bread into small pieces. It's best to use a firm bread that is a couple of days old. Fresh, soft bread will give you a stuffing that is too moist and soggy.

Ingredient Substitution

To add a little sweetness to this stuffing, add 1 1/2 cups chopped apples and 1/2 cup raisins with the pecans.

Serving Suggestion

A delicious meatless second meal can be made from any leftover stuffing. Simply shape the stuffing into patties, and heat in margarine until brown on both sides. Serve with your favorite green veggie and juicy tomato slices.

4 cups soft bread crumbs (about 6 slices bread)

1 cup crushed saltine crackers (about eighteen 2-inch squares)

1 cup chopped pecans

1 large onion, chopped (1 cup)

2 medium stalks celery, chopped (1 cup)

2/3 cup vegetable or chicken broth

1/2 cup fat-free cholesterol-free egg product

1/4 cup margarine or butter, melted

1/2 teaspoon pepper

1/2 teaspoon rubbed sage

Chopped fresh parsley, if desired

1. Spray inside of 2- to 3 1/2-quart slow cooker with cooking spray.

2. Mix bread crumbs, cracker crumbs, pecans, onion and celery in cooker.

3. Mix remaining ingredients except parsley; pour into cooker. Toss to coat ingredients.

4. Cover and cook on low heat setting 4 to 5 hours or until stuffing is slightly puffed and brown around the edges.

5. Sprinkle with parsley.

1 Serving: Calories 405 (Calories from Fat 180); Fat 20g (Saturated 3g); Cholesterol 0mg; Sodium 720mg; Carbohydrate 49g (Dietary Fiber 3g); Protein 10g

% Daily Value: Vitamin A 10%; Vitamin C 2%; Calcium 14%; Iron 24%

Diet Exchanges: 3 Starch, 4 Fat

Carrot and Celery Relish

▪ 2 1/2 cups relish ▪

SLOW COOKER:
2- to 3 1/2-quart

PREP TIME:
20 minutes

COOK TIME:
High 2 to 2 1/2 hours

FINISHING COOK TIME:
High 15 minutes

Ingredient Substitution

We like the added color and flavor of the green bell pepper, but you can use any color pepper you like—red, yellow or orange.

Serving Suggestion

Spark up the taste of a plain hot dog or hamburger by spooning on this colorful relish. Or stir a few tablespoons into fat-free mayonnaise, and use it to dress up a crisp tossed salad.

4 to 5 medium carrots, coarsely shredded (2 1/2 cups)

4 medium stalks celery, sliced (2 cups)

1 small green bell pepper, chopped (1/2 cup)

2/3 cup sugar

1/2 cup white vinegar

2 teaspoons salt

1 teaspoon celery seed

2 teaspoons cornstarch

2 teaspoons cold water

1. Mix all ingredients except cornstarch and water in 2- to 3 1/2-quart slow cooker.

2. Cover and cook on high heat setting 2 to 2 1/2 hours or until vegetables are tender.

3. Mix cornstarch and water; stir into vegetable mixture.

4. Cover and cook on high heat setting about 15 minutes or until thickened. Cool about 2 hours.

5. Spoon relish into container. Cover and store in refrigerator up to 3 weeks.

1 Tablespoon: Calories 20 (Calories from Fat 0); Fat 0g (Saturated 0g); Cholesterol 0mg; Sodium 125mg; Carbohydrate 5g (Dietary Fiber 0g); Protein 0g

% Daily Value: Vitamin A 10%; Vitamin C 2%; Calcium 0%; Iron 0%

Diet Exchanges: 1 Vegetable

Date:

CARROT &
CELERY
RELISH

Corn Relish

3 cups relish

SLOW COOKER:
2- to 3 1/2-quart

PREP TIME:
15 minutes

COOK TIME:
High 2 to 2 1/2 hours

FINISHING COOK TIME:
High 15 to 20 minutes

Ingredient Substitution

If you have ketchup but no chili sauce, feel free to use it. It'll work just as well in this relish.

Finishing Touch

For a Mexican corn relish, stir in a rinsed and drained 15-ounce can of black beans and a drained small can of chopped green chilies before refrigerating.

1 bag (16 ounces) frozen whole kernel corn

1 medium bell pepper, chopped (1 cup)

1 medium onion, chopped (1/2 cup)

1/3 cup sugar

1/3 cup chili sauce

1/3 cup white vinegar

1 teaspoon salt

1/2 teaspoon celery seed

1 teaspoon cornstarch

2 teaspoons cold water

1. Rinse corn with cold water to separate kernels and remove ice crystals. Mix corn and remaining ingredients except cornstarch and water in 2- to 3 1/2-quart slow cooker.

2. Cover and cook on high heat setting 2 to 2 1/2 hours or until vegetables are tender.

3. Mix cornstarch and water; stir into corn mixture.

4. Cover and cook on high heat setting 15 to 20 minutes or until thickened. Cool about 2 hours.

5. Spoon relish into container. Cover and store in refrigerator up to 3 weeks.

1 Tablespoon: Calories 20 (Calories from Fat 0); Fat 0g (Saturated 0g); Cholesterol 0mg; Sodium 70mg; Carbohydrate 4g (Dietary Fiber 0g); Protein 0g

% Daily Value: Vitamin A 2%; Vitamin C 4%; Calcium 0%; Iron 0%

Diet Exchanges: 1 Vegetable

Golden Fruit Chutney

■ 4 1/2 cups chutney ■

SLOW COOKER:
2- to 3 1/2-quart

PREP TIME:
15 minutes

COOK TIME:
Low 6 to 8 hours

Ingredient Substitution

Dried peaches or dried apples can be used instead of the apricots. You may want to try dark raisins or dried cranberries with the dried apples.

Serving Suggestion

For an easy appetizer, spoon about a cup of chutney over a softened 8-ounce package of cream cheese. Sprinkle with chopped peanuts and chopped green onions. Serve with crackers to spread it on.

1 can (20 ounces) pineapple chunks in juice or syrup, undrained

2 packages (6 ounces each) dried apricots, coarsely chopped (2 cups)

1 cup golden raisins

1/2 cup packed brown sugar

1/2 cup cider vinegar

1 1/2 teaspoons ground ginger

1 teaspoon ground mustard (dry)

1/8 teaspoon ground red pepper (cayenne)

1. Mix all ingredients in 2- to 3 1/2-quart slow cooker.

2. Cover and cook on low heat setting 6 to 8 hours or until very thick. Cool about 2 hours.

3. Spoon chutney into container. Cover and store in refrigerator up to 3 weeks or in freezer up to 2 months.

1 Tablespoon: Calories 20 (Calories from Fat 0); Fat 0g (Saturated 0g); Cholesterol 0mg; Sodium 0mg; Carbohydrate 5g (Dietary Fiber 0g); Protein 0g

% Daily Value: Vitamin A 0%; Vitamin C 0%; Calcium 0%; Iron 0%

Diet Exchanges: 1/2 Fruit

Peach-Cherry Chutney

■ 2 1/2 cups chutney ■

SLOW COOKER:
2- to 3 1/2-quart

PREP TIME:
15 minutes

COOK TIME:
Low 6 to 8 hours

2 cans (15 1/4 ounces each) sliced peaches, well drained and chopped

1/2 cup sugar

1/3 cup dried cherries

1/3 cup cider vinegar

2 teaspoons finely chopped jalapeño chili

1 teaspoon grated gingerroot

1/2 teaspoon ground allspice

1/2 cup chopped red onion

1. Mix all ingredients in 2- to 3 1/2-quart slow cooker.

2. Cover and cook on low heat setting 6 to 8 hours or until very thick. Cool about 2 hours.

3. Spoon chutney into container. Cover and store in refrigerator up to 3 weeks.

Betty's Success Tip

Here's an easy way to remove the thin, paperlike peel from fresh gingerroot: Scrape it with the side of a spoon. Grating the gingerroot will give you a thick, juicy, aromatic pulp.

Ingredient Substitution

If you prefer, use a teaspoon of ground ginger in place of the grated fresh gingerroot. Also, you can use dried cranberries or raisins if dried cherries aren't available.

1 Tablespoon: Calories 20 (Calories from Fat 0); Fat 0g (Saturated 0g); Cholesterol 0mg; Sodium 0mg; Carbohydrate 6g (Dietary Fiber 1g); Protein 0g

% Daily Value: Vitamin A 0%; Vitamin C 2%; Calcium 0%; Iron 0%

Diet Exchanges: 1 Vegetable

Peach-Cherry Chutney ➤

Pear-Orange Conserve

■ 4 cups conserve ■

SLOW COOKER:
2- to 3 1/2-quart

PREP TIME:
20 minutes

COOK TIME:
High 2 hours

UNCOVERED COOK TIME:
High 1 1/2 to 2 hours

5 medium pears, cored and diced (6 cups)

1 medium orange, seeded and chopped

1 1/2 cups sugar

1/2 cup chopped maraschino cherries

1/2 cup chopped walnuts

1. Mix pears, orange and sugar in 2- to 3 1/2-quart slow cooker.

2. Cover and cook on high heat setting 2 hours.

3. Stir mixture. Cook uncovered on high heat setting 1 1/2 to 2 hours or until very thick. Stir in cherries and walnuts. Cool about 2 hours.

4. Spoon conserve into container. Cover and store in refrigerator up to 3 weeks.

1 Tablespoon: Calories 40 (Calories from Fat 10); Fat 1g (Saturated 0g); Cholesterol 0mg; Sodium 0mg; Carbohydrate 8g (Dietary Fiber 0g); Protein 0g

% Daily Value: Vitamin A 0%; Vitamin C 0%; Calcium 0%; Iron 0%

Diet Exchanges: 1/2 Fruit

Betty's Success Tip

There is no need to peel the orange before chopping it because the peel will crystallize due to the slow cooking and amount of sugar. The peel also gives the conserve a wonderful orange flavor.

Serving Suggestion

A conserve is a type of preserves that contains two or more fruits and some type of nut. It usually is used as a spread for toast, biscuits, scones and bread. The orange flavor of this conserve, however, makes it a tasty accompaniment to serve with pork, ham, chicken, turkey and duck—both wild and domestic.

Pear-Orange Conserve ➤

Curried Fruit

■ *12 servings* ■

SLOW COOKER:
3 1/2- to 6-quart

PREP TIME:
10 minutes

COOK TIME:
Low 3 to 4 hours

Ingredient Substitution

If you prefer, use 3 cans of apricot halves, sliced peaches or sliced pears with the pineapple and cherries.

Serving Suggestion

Curried fruit has many uses; you might be surprised how often you make it. It is a delicious side dish with any type of meat—pork, lamb, ham, turkey or chicken. Use it to top pancakes or waffles at your next weekend breakfast. For dessert, top bowls of chilled curried fruit with plain yogurt and a sprinkle of toasted coconut.

Finishing Touch

Enhance the curry flavor and the tender fruit by stirring 1/2 cup toasted slivered almonds into the curried fruit before serving, or sprinkle them on top.

1 can (20 ounces) pineapple chunks in juice or syrup, drained

1 can (15 1/4 ounces) sliced pears, drained

1 can (15 1/4 ounces) sliced peaches, drained

1 can (15 1/4 ounces) apricot halves, drained

1/2 cup maraschino cherries, drained

2/3 cup packed brown sugar

1/3 cup margarine or butter, melted

2 to 3 teaspoons curry powder

1. Arrange pineapple, pears, peaches, apricots and cherries in 3 1/2- to 6-quart slow cooker. Mix remaining ingredients; spoon over fruit.

2. Cover and cook on low heat setting 3 to 4 hours to develop the flavors.

3. Serve warm or chilled. To chill, cool about 2 hours, then spoon fruit into container; cover and refrigerate until chilled.

1 Serving: Calories 180 (Calories from Fat 45); Fat 5g (Saturated 1g); Cholesterol omg; Sodium 80mg; Carbohydrate 35g (Dietary Fiber 2g); Protein 10g

% Daily Value: Vitamin A 12%; Vitamin C 8%; Calcium 2%; Iron 4%

Diet Exchanges: 2 1/2 Fruit, 1 Fat

Apple Butter

▪ 4 cups apple butter ▪

SLOW COOKER:
5- to 6-quart

PREP TIME:
30 minutes

COOK TIME:
Low 8 to 10 hours

UNCOVERED COOK TIME:
Low 1 to 2 hours

Betty's Success Tip

We used a tart cooking apple, but if you prefer a sweeter cooking apple such as Beacon or Prairie Spy, you may want to use only 1 1/4 cups packed brown sugar. Apple butter should be pleasantly sweet with a spicy flavor.

Ingredient Substitution

Not only will you enjoy this wonderful apple butter, but also your house will smell delicious while it is cooking! You can use apple cider or water instead of the apple juice. For "spirited" apple butter, use 1/4 cup apple brandy and 1/4 apple juice or apple cider.

Serving Suggestion

Even though this thick mixture has no butter, its name comes from the fact that it spreads like butter. Spread your favorite bagel with cream cheese and spicy apple butter. Use it instead of butter on hot toast, English muffins or freshly baked biscuits or scones. Or spoon it on top of a stack of hot pancakes or waffles, and sprinkle with chopped toasted pecans.

12 medium Granny Smith or other cooking apples, peeled, cored and cut into fourths

1 1/2 cups packed dark or light brown sugar

1/2 cup apple juice

1 tablespoon ground cinnamon

1 tablespoon lemon juice

1 teaspoon ground allspice

1 teaspoon ground nutmeg

1/2 teaspoon ground cloves

1. Mix all ingredients in 5- to 6-quart slow cooker.

2. Cover and cook on low heat setting 8 to 10 hours or until apples are very tender.

3. Mash apples with potato masher or large fork.

4. Cook uncovered on low heat setting 1 to 2 hours, stirring occasionally, until mixture is very thick. Cool about 2 hours.

5. Spoon apple butter into container. Cover and store in refrigerator up to 3 weeks.

1 Tablespoon: Calories 30(Calories from Fat 0); Fat 0g (Saturated 0g); Cholesterol 0mg; Sodium 0mg; Carbohydrate 9 (Dietary Fiber 1); Protein 0g

% Daily Value: Vitamin A 0%; Vitamin C 2; Calcium 0%; Iron 0%

Diet Exchanges: 1/2 Fruit

Beginnings and Endings

◄ *Artichoke-Crab Spread (page 192), Spiced Cran-Apple
Cider (page 193)*

185

Cheese-Beer Dip

■ 2 1/2 cups dip ■

SLOW COOKER:
1- to 2 1/2-quart

PREP TIME:
10 minutes

COOK TIME:
High 35 to 45 minutes

HOLD TIME:
Low up to 4 hours

1 package (16 ounces) process cheese spread loaf, cut into pieces

1/2 cup regular or nonalcoholic beer

1/2 to 1 teaspoon red pepper sauce

Bread cubes, pretzel nuggets or bite-size pieces fresh vegetables, if desired

1. Spray inside of 1- to 2 1/2-quart slow cooker with cooking spray.

2. Mix cheese, beer and pepper sauce in cooker.

3. Cover and cook on high heat setting 35 to 45 minutes or until cheese is melted. Stir until cheese is smooth.

4. Scrape down side of cooker with rubber spatula to help prevent edge of dip from scorching. Turn to low heat setting.

5. Serve with bread cubes and wooden picks or fondue forks for dipping. Dip will hold up to 4 hours.

1 Tablespoon: Calories 50 (Calories from Fat 35); Fat 4g (Saturated 4g); Cholesterol 2mg; Sodium 160mg; Carbohydrate 4g (Dietary Fiber 0g); Protein 3g

% Daily Value: Vitamin A 2%; Vitamin C 0%; Calcium 6%; Iron 0%

Diet Exchanges: 1 Fat

Betty's Success Tip

This is the perfect cheese dip for a party because it will stay smooth and creamy for 4 hours—if it lasts that long! The process cheese spread loaf not only is easy to melt but also doesn't curdle or separate while standing. Just stir the dip occasionally so that a thin film doesn't form on the top.

Ingredient Substitution

If you want to add a little more color and zip to this dip, use process cheese spread loaf with jalapeño peppers. You may not want to add the red pepper sauce. Taste the dip first without it and then decide how hot you want to make it.

Serving Suggestion

Double this recipe if you ran out too soon the last time you served it. Have leftover dip? Heat it the next day, and serve over toast with slices of ripe, juicy tomatoes for lunch. It also makes a great topper for steamed veggies, too.

Cheesy Bean Dip

■ 3 1/2 cups dip ■

SLOW COOKER:
2- to 3 1/2-quart

PREP TIME:
10 minutes

COOK TIME:
High 30 to 40 minutes

HOLD TIME:
Low up to 4 hours

Serving Suggestion

Having a large party? Borrow another small slow cooker, and make two dips. You can place one at each end of the buffet table or at two different places, so they will be easier for guests to reach. Or double the recipe to be sure you have enough during the party.

Finishing Touch

Sprinkle the top of the dip with chopped fresh cilantro just before serving. The cool mint flavor of cilantro will complement the chilies in this dip. For a more festive presentation, use a variety of colored tortilla chips, such as white, yellow and blue cornmeal chips. Red and green chips also are available during the holidays.

1 package (16 ounces) process cheese spread loaf with jalapeño peppers, cut into cubes

1 can (15 or 16 ounces) refried beans

1 can (4 ounces) chopped green chilies, undrained

Tortilla chips, if desired

1. Spray inside of 2- to 3 1/2-quart slow cooker with cooking spray.

2. Mix cheese, beans and chilies in cooker.

3. Cover and cook on high heat setting 30 to 40 minutes or until cheese is melted. Stir until cheese is smooth.

4. Scrape down side of cooker with rubber spatula to help prevent edge of dip from scorching. Turn to low heat setting.

5. Serve with tortilla chips. Dip will hold up to 4 hours.

1 Tablespoon: Calories 40 (Calories from Fat 25); Fat 3g (Saturated 2g); Cholesterol 10mg; Sodium 140mg; Carbohydrate 1g (Dietary Fiber 0g); Protein 2g

% Daily Value: Vitamin A 2%; Vitamin C 0%; Calcium 4%; Iron 0%

Diet Exchanges: 1 Fat

Pizza Fondue

■ *6 cups fondue* ■

SLOW COOKER:
2- to 3 1/2-quart

PREP TIME:
10 minutes

COOK TIME:
High 45 to 60 minutes

HOLD TIME:
Low up to 4 hours

Ingredient Substitution

Varying this cheesy fondue is so easy by using your favorite spaghetti sauce, such as garden vegetable or mushroom and ripe olive.

Serving Suggestion

Need an easy meal your family will love? Pizza Fondue is the answer for a great weekend meatless meal. Put the fondue on hold while you and the family go to a movie or attend the kids' softball game. When you arrive home, make a quick Caesar salad using a bag of salad mix, and you are ready to eat.

1 package (16 ounces) process cheese spread loaf, cut into cubes

2 cups shredded mozzarella cheese (8 ounces)

1 jar (28 ounces) spaghetti sauce

1/2 cup dry red wine or beef broth

1 loaf Italian bread, cut into 1-inch cubes, for serving, if desired

1. Spray inside of 2- to 3 1/2-quart slow cooker with cooking spray.

2. Mix cheeses, spaghetti sauce and wine in cooker.

3. Cover and cook on high heat setting 45 to 60 minutes or until cheese is melted. Stir until cheese is smooth.

4. Scrape down side of cooker with rubber spatula to help prevent edge of fondue from scorching. Turn to low heat setting.

5. Serve with bread cubes and wooden picks or fondue forks for dipping. Fondue will hold up to 4 hours.

1 Tablespoon: Calories 30 (Calories from Fat 20); Fat 2g (Saturated 1g); Cholesterol 5mg; Sodium 120mg; Carbohydrate 2g (Dietary Fiber 0g); Protein 2g

% Daily Value: Vitamin A 2%; Vitamin C 0%; Calcium 4%; Iron 0%

Diet Exchanges: 1 Vegetable, 1 Fat

Pizza Fondue ➤

Hot Reuben Spread

■ *3 1/4 cups spread* ■

SLOW COOKER:
1- to 2 1/2-quart

PREP TIME:
10 minutes

COOK TIME:
Low 1 to 1 1/2 hours

HOLD TIME:
Low up to 4 hours

Betty's Success Tip

Sauerkraut sometimes can be quite salty. Rinsing it in a strainer under cold water can help remove some of the salty flavor.

Serving Suggestion

You don't have to throw a party to enjoy a Reuben spread sandwich. Toast slices of rye or pumpernickel bread. Spread about 1/2 cup Reuben spread over each slice. Pop the open-face sandwiches under the broiler until the tops are hot and bubbly and begin to brown. Serve with big, crisp dill pickles—just like at your favorite deli restaurant!

1 package (8 ounces) cream cheese, softened

2 packages (2 1/2 ounces each) thinly sliced corned beef, chopped

1 1/2 cups shredded Swiss cheese (6 ounces)

3/4 cup drained sauerkraut

1/2 cup Thousand Island dressing

Pretzel crackers or cocktail rye bread slices, for serving, if desired

1. Spray inside of 1- to 2 1/2-quart slow cooker with cooking spray.

2. Mix all ingredients except crackers; spoon into cooker.

3. Cover and cook on low heat setting 1 to 1 1/2 hours or until cheese is melted. Stir until cheese is smooth.

4. Scrape down side of cooker with rubber spatula to help prevent edge of spread from scorching. Turn to low heat setting.

5. Serve with crackers. Spread will hold up to 4 hours.

1 Tablespoon: Calories 40 (Calories from Fat 25); Fat 3g (Saturated 2g); Cholesterol 10mg; Sodium 100mg; Carbohydrate 1g (Dietary Fiber 0g); Protein 2g

% Daily Value: Vitamin A 2%; Vitamin C 0%; Calcium 4%; Iron 0%

Diet Exchanges: 1 Fat

Hot Reuben Spread ➤

Artichoke-Crab Spread

■ 3 cups spread ■

SLOW COOKER:
1- to 2 1/2-quart

PREP TIME:
15 minutes

COOK TIME:
Low 1 to 1 1/4 hours
High 30 to 45 minutes

HOLD TIME:
Low up to 3 hours

1 can (14 ounces) artichoke heart quarters, drained and coarsely chopped

1 package (8 ounces) cream cheese, cubed

4 medium green onions, sliced (1/4 cup)

1 cup shredded imitation crabmeat (4 ounces)

1/2 cup grated Parmesan cheese

4 teaspoons lemon juice

French baguette or cocktail rye bread slices, for serving, if desired

1. Spray inside of 1- to 2 1/2-quart slow cooker with cooking spray.

2. Place all ingredients except bread in cooker.

3. Cover and cook on low heat setting 1 to 1 1/4 hours (or high heat setting 30 to 45 minutes) or until cream cheese is melted. Stir until cheese is smooth.

4. Scrape down side of cooker with rubber spatula to help prevent edge of spread from scorching. Turn to low heat setting.

5. Serve with bread slices. Spread will hold up to 3 hours.

1 Tablespoon: Calories 25 (Calories from Fat 20); Fat 2g (Saturated 1g); Cholesterol 5mg; Sodium 80mg; Carbohydrate 1g (Dietary Fiber 0g); Protein 1g

% Daily Value: Vitamin A 2%; Vitamin C 0%; Calcium 2%; Iron 0%

Diet Exchanges: 1/2 Fat

Betty's Success Tip

Everyone will love this delicious, rich spread. Because of the richness of the cheeses, however, the spread may start to separate, and little puddles could appear on the surface. So stir the spread occasionally, and it will look as good as new.

Ingredient Substitution

Fresh crabmeat isn't available to everyone all year around, so that is why we suggest using the imitation crabmeat. The shredded imitation crabmeat for salad is perfect for this dip. But you can use drained canned crabmeat, or if you are fortunate, use shredded cooked fresh crabmeat.

Spiced Cran-Apple Cider

■ 24 servings (1/2 cup each) ■

SLOW COOKER:
3 1/2- to 6-quart

PREP TIME:
5 minutes

COOK TIME:
Low 4 to 6 hours

1 bottle (48 ounces) apple cider (6 cups)

1 bottle (48 ounces) cranberry juice cocktail (6 cups)

1/3 cup packed brown sugar

2 teaspoons whole allspice

4 sticks cinnamon, 3 inches long

1. Mix all ingredients in 3 1/2- to 6-quart slow cooker.

2. Cover and cook on low heat setting 4 to 6 hours. Remove allspice and cinnamon before serving.

1 Serving: Calories 80 (Calories from Fat 0); Fat 0g (Saturated 0g); Cholesterol 0mg; Sodium 0mg; Carbohydrate 20g (Dietary Fiber 0g); Protein 0g

% Daily Value: Vitamin A 0%; Vitamin C 18%; Calcium 0%; Iron 2%

Diet Exchanges: 1 1/2 Fruit

Betty's Success Tip

Tying the allspice and cinnamon in a cheesecloth bag makes them easy to remove from the hot cider. Or if you don't have cheesecloth, place the spices in a paper coffee filter and tie with a piece of kitchen string.

Finishing Touch

Fresh orange slices add a pretty touch of color to this ruby-red hot drink. Add them to the cider in the cooker just before serving.

Mocha Cocoa

◾ *12 servings (1 cup each)* ◾

SLOW COOKER:
5- to 6-quart
PREP TIME:
5 minutes
COOK TIME:
Low 3 to 4 hours

Ingredient Substitution

Just leave out the coffee and cinnamon to make this recipe more kid friendly. After all, what's a winter party for kids without hot cocoa? Serve it with plenty of marshmallows to float on top, or stick a candy cane into each mug of cocoa.

Serving Suggestion

This recipe is easy to cut in half for a treat for the family. Just use 2 1/2 cups dry milk, 1/2 cup cocoa, 1/3 cup sugar, 5 1/2 cups water and 1 teaspoon vanilla in a 2- to 3 1/2-quart slow cooker. You can decide whether you want to include 2 tablespoons instant coffee and 1/4 teaspoon cinnamon.

5 cups nonfat dry milk

1 cup baking cocoa

3/4 cup sugar

1/4 cup instant coffee (dry)

1/2 teaspoon ground cinnamon

11 cups water

2 teaspoons vanilla

1. Mix all ingredients except water and vanilla in 5- to 6-quart slow cooker. Stir in water and vanilla until smooth.

2. Cover and cook on low heat setting 3 to 4 hours.

1 Serving: Calories 170 (Calories from Fat 10); Fat 1g (Saturated 1g); Cholesterol 5mg; Sodium 160mg; Carbohydrate 32g (Dietary Fiber 3g); Protein 11g

% Daily Value: Vitamin A 20%; Vitamin C 0%; Calcium 36%; Iron 6%

Diet Exchanges: 1 Starch, 1 Skim Milk

Wassail

16 servings (1/2 cup each)

Crowd
SIZE

SLOW COOKER:
3 1/2- to 6-quart

PREP TIME:
5 minutes

COOK TIME:
Low 3 to 4 hours

Betty's Success Tip

Removing the spices will be easy if you tie them in a cheesecloth bag or a paper coffee filter. If you don't have either cheesecloth or a coffee filter, just use a spoon to "fish" out the spices.

Ingredient Substitution

You can use this recipe to make a delicious hot apple cider. Just use 8 cups of apple cider and no red wine. Can't you just smell that wonderful spicy apple aroma?

Serving Suggestion

Serve this robust punch during the winter holidays, and salute your friends and family with the toast, "Wassail." Wassail combines Old English and Old Icelandic phrases meaning "good health and fortune."

5 cups apple cider

3 cups dry red wine

1/4 cup granulated or packed brown sugar

1/2 teaspoon whole cloves

1/4 teaspoon whole allspice

1 stick cinnamon, 3 inches long

1. Mix all ingredients in 3 1/2- to 6-quart slow cooker.

2. Cover and cook on low heat setting 3 to 4 hours. Remove cloves, allspice and cinnamon before serving.

1 Serving: Calories 80 (Calories from Fat 0); Fat 0g (Saturated 0g); Cholesterol 0mg; Sodium 5mg; Carbohydrate 13g (Dietary Fiber 0g); Protein 0g

% Daily Value: Vitamin A 0%; Vitamin C 0%; Calcium 0%; Iron 2%

Diet Exchanges: 1 Fruit

Butterscotch-Rum Dip

■ 3 cups dip ■

SLOW COOKER:
1- to 2 1/2-quart

PREP TIME:
10 minutes

COOK TIME:
Low 45 to 60 minutes

HOLD TIME:
Low up to 2 hours

Ingredient Substitution

Rum and butterscotch flavors blend nicely together. If you prefer not to use rum, however, add 2 teaspoons of rum extract. Or you can leave out the rum to make a delicious, nutty butterscotch dip—the choice is yours.

Serving Suggestion

Leftover dip? No problem. It keeps well in the refrigerator. Warm it and serve with pancakes or waffles. Top a slice of apple pie, pound cake or angel food cake with a scoop of ice cream, and pour warm butterscotch sauce over the top. In fact, this dip is so delicious, you might just want to make a batch to keep on hand.

2 packages (11 ounces each) butterscotch-flavored chips (4 cups total)

2/3 cup evaporated milk

2/3 cup walnuts, toasted (page 152) and finely chopped

2 tablespoons rum

Apple and pear wedges, for serving, if desired

1. Mix butterscotch chips and evaporated milk in 1- to 2 1/2-quart slow cooker.

2. Cover and cook on low heat setting 45 to 60 minutes or until chips are melted. Stir until mixture is smooth. Stir in walnuts and rum.

3. Serve with apple and pear wedges. Dip will hold up to 2 hours.

1 Tablespoon: Calories 90 (Calories from Fat 45); Fat 5g (Saturated 4g); Cholesterol 0mg; Sodium 15mg; Carbohydrate 10g (Dietary Fiber 0g); Protein 1g

% Daily Value: Vitamin A 0%; Vitamin C 0%; Calcium 2%; Iron 0%

Diet Exchanges: 1/2 Starch, 1 Fat

Chocolate Fondue

■ 2 1/4 cups fondue ■

SLOW COOKER:
1- to 2 1/2-quart

PREP TIME:
5 minutes

COOK TIME:
Low 45 to 60 minutes

HOLD TIME:
Low 2 hours

1 package (12 ounces) semisweet chocolate chips (2 cups)

1/2 cup half-and-half

1 to 3 tablespoons orange-flavored liqueur, if desired

Fruit Dippers (below), for serving, if desired

1. Mix chocolate chips and half-and-half in 1- to 2 1/2-quart slow cooker.

2. Cover and cook on low heat setting 45 to 60 minutes or until chocolate is melted. Stir until mixture is smooth. Stir in liqueur.

3. Serve with Fruit Dippers and wooden picks or fondue forks for dipping. Fondue will hold up to 2 hours.

Fruit Dippers

Select one or several of the following fruits: apple wedges, banana slices, kiwifruit wedges, melon balls, fresh or mandarin orange sections, pear wedges, pineapple chunks, strawberries. Dip apple wedges, banana slices and pear wedges in lemon or pineapple juice to help prevent them from turning dark.

1 Tablespoon: Calories 55 (Calories from Fat 25); Fat 3g (Saturated 2g); Cholesterol 0mg; Sodium 0mg; Carbohydrate 6g (Dietary Fiber 0g); Protein 1g

% Daily Value: Vitamin A 0%; Vitamin C 0%; Calcium 0%; Iron 2%

Diet Exchanges: 1/2 Fruit, 1/2 Fat

Ingredient Substitution

You can use any chocolate you have on hand—chocolate chips, mint-chocolate chips or white baking chips. For a flavor twist, use any fruit-flavored liqueur; coffee-, almond- or ginger-flavored liqueur; white crème de menthe; brandy or rum—the choices are endless. For the kids, make this fun-to-eat fondue with peanut butter chips or butterscotch-flavored chips.

Serving Suggestion

Chocolate makes anything taste sensational! Cubes of pound or angel food cake, large marshmallows, pretzels or rippled potato chips are a few more dipper ideas. What do you think would be good dipped in chocolate?

Finishing Touch

Place dishes of toasted coconut and chopped toasted nuts next to the fondue. Dip a piece of fruit into the chocolate, then into the coconut or nuts for the ultimate taste treat.

Hot Fudge Sundae Cake

■ *6 servings* ■

SLOW COOKER:
2- to 3 1/2-quart

PREP TIME:
15 minutes

COOK TIME:
High 2 to 2 1/2 hours

COOL TIME:
30 to 40 minutes

1 cup all-purpose flour

1/2 cup granulated sugar

2 tablespoons baking cocoa

2 teaspoons baking powder

1/2 teaspoon salt

1/2 cup milk

2 tablespoons vegetable oil

1 teaspoon vanilla

1/2 cup chopped nuts

3/4 cup packed brown sugar

1/4 cup baking cocoa

1 1/2 cups hot water

Betty's Success Tip

We found that if you let the cake cool in the cooker before serving it, the sauce under the cake will thicken to a good consistency. If you eat it sooner, the sauce will be thinner but still delicious.

Finishing Touch

For a special treat, add 1/3 cup halved maraschino cherries with the nuts. Top with a scoop of your favorite ice cream. Tuck a long-stemmed maraschino cherry on top each serving to make this the best-ever sundae cake.

1. Spray inside of 2- to 3 1/2-quart slow cooker with cooking spray.

2. Mix flour, granulated sugar, 2 tablespoons cocoa, the baking powder and salt in medium bowl. Stir in milk, oil and vanilla until smooth. Stir in nuts. Spread batter evenly in bottom of cooker.

3. Mix brown sugar and 1/4 cup cocoa in small bowl. Stir in hot water until smooth. Pour evenly over batter in cooker.

4. Cover and cook on high heat setting 2 to 2 1/2 hours or until toothpick inserted in center comes out clean.

5. Turn off cooker. Let cake stand uncovered 30 to 40 minutes to cool slightly before serving.

6. Spoon warm cake into dessert dishes. Spoon sauce over top.

1 Serving: Calories 380 (Calories from Fat 110); Fat 12g (Saturated 2g); Cholesterol 0mg; Sodium 380mg; Carbohydrate 66g (Dietary Fiber 3g); Protein 5g

% Daily Value: Vitamin A 0%; Vitamin C 0%; Calcium 16%; Iron 14%

Diet Exchanges: Not recommended

Cherry Cobbler

■ *6 servings* ■

SLOW COOKER:
2- to 3 1/2-quart

PREP TIME:
10 minutes

COOK TIME:
High 1 1/2 to 2 hours

Ingredient Substitution

Life is just a bowl of cherries—cobbler, that is. But peach, apple, blueberry or raspberry pie filling also would make a luscious cobbler. For a little extra crunch, stir 1/4 cup toasted nuts into the batter before spreading over the pie filling—yummy.

Finishing Touch

Pass a pitcher of heavy whipping cream, half-and-half or eggnog, when it is available, to pour over bowls of warm cobbler. Sprinkle a little ground cinnamon or nutmeg on top for just a hint of spiciness.

1 can (21 ounces) cherry pie filling

1 cup all-purpose flour

1/4 cup sugar

1/4 cup margarine or butter, melted

1/2 cup milk

1 1/2 teaspoons baking powder

1/2 teaspoon almond extract

1/4 teaspoon salt

1. Spray inside of 2- to 3 1/2-quart slow cooker with cooking spray.

2. Pour pie filling into cooker.

3. Beat remaining ingredients with spoon until smooth. Spread batter over pie filling.

4. Cover and cook on high heat setting 1 1/2 to 2 hours or until toothpick inserted in center comes out clean.

1 Serving: Calories 270 (Calories from Fat 70); Fat 8g (Saturated 2g); Cholesterol 0mg; Sodium 330mg; Carbohydrate 49g (Dietary Fiber 2g); Protein 3g

% Daily Value: Vitamin A 12%; Vitamin C 0%; Calcium 10%; Iron 6%

Diet Exchanges: 1 Starch, 2 Fruit, 1 1/2 Fat

Cherry Cobbler ➤

Blackberry Dumplings

■ 6 servings ■

SLOW COOKER:
3 1/2- or 4-quart

PREP TIME:
10 minutes

COOK TIME:
Low 3 to 4 hours
High 1 1/2 to 2 hours

FINISHING COOK TIME:
20 to 25 minutes

Betty's Success Tip

For light, fluffy dumplings, be sure the berry mixture is boiling before dropping the dough on top. If the mixture isn't hot enough, the tops of the dumplings will be wet and doughy. Dumplings need steam to rise during cooking, so don't lift the cover and peek because the steam will sneak out.

Ingredient Substitution

Any type of fresh or frozen berries can be used in this recipe. Try blueberries, strawberries, raspberries or a combination of two or three. If you use frozen berries, be sure to buy the bag of berries that aren't frozen in syrup.

1 package (14 ounces) frozen blackberries (3 cups), thawed and drained

1/3 cup sugar

1/3 cup water

1 teaspoon lemon juice

1 cup Bisquick Original baking mix

2 tablespoons sugar

1/3 cup milk

Ground cinnamon

Whipping (heavy) cream or vanilla ice cream, if desired

1. Mix blackberries, 1/3 cup sugar, the water and lemon juice in 3 1/2- or 4-quart slow cooker.

2. Cover and cook on low heat setting 3 to 4 hours (or high heat setting 1 1/2 to 2 hours) or until mixture is boiling.

3. Mix baking mix and 2 tablespoons sugar in small bowl. Stir in milk just until dry ingredients are moistened. Drop dough by 6 spoonfuls onto hot berry mixture. Sprinkle with cinnamon.

4. Cover and cook on high heat setting 20 to 25 minutes or until toothpick inserted in center of dumplings comes out clean.

5. To serve, spoon dumpling into dessert dish. Spoon berry mixture over dumpling. Top with whipping cream.

1 Serving: Calories 165 (Calories from Fat 25); Fat 3g (Saturated 1g); Cholesterol omg; Sodium 290mg; Carbohydrate 37g (Dietary Fiber 4g); Protein 2g

% Daily Value: Vitamin A 2%; Vitamin C 12%; Calcium 8%; Iron 6%

Diet Exchanges: 1 Starch, 1 1/2 Fruit

Cranberry Baked Apples

■ *4 servings* ■

SLOW COOKER:
5- to 6-quart

PREP TIME:
15 minutes

COOK TIME:
Low 4 to 6 hours

4 large cooking apples

1/3 cup packed brown sugar

1/4 cup dried cranberries

1/2 cup cran-apple juice cocktail

2 tablespoons margarine or butter, melted

1/2 teaspoon ground cinnamon

1/4 teaspoon ground nutmeg

Chopped nuts, if desired

1. Core apples. Fill centers of apples with brown sugar and cranberries. Place apples in 5- to 6-quart slow cooker.

2. Mix cran-apple juice and margarine; pour over apples. Sprinkle with cinnamon and nutmeg.

3. Cover and cook on low heat setting 4 to 6 hours or until apples are tender.

4. To serve, spoon apples into dessert dishes. Spoon sauce over apples. Sprinkle with nuts.

Betty's Success Tip

We like to use a cooking apple that will hold its shape after it is cooked. Good selections are Rome Beauty, Golden Delicious, Beacon, San Rose and Wealthy apples. Granny Smith apples also are an excellent cooking apple, but they are quite tart, so you may want to increase the sugar a tablespoon.

Ingredient Substitution

Dried cranberries are a natural with apples, but other dried fruits are just as tasty. Try dried cherries, mixed dried fruits or dark or golden raisins for a flavor change.

Finishing Touch

Like apple pie with Cheddar cheese? Sprinkle these hot baked apples with shredded Cheddar cheese instead of the nuts. It's like eating apple pie but with fewer calories because there is no crust.

1 Serving: Calories 285 (Calories from Fat 65); Fat 7g (Saturated 1g); Cholesterol 0mg; Sodium 85mg; Carbohydrate 63g (Dietary Fiber 9g); Protein 1g

% Daily Value: Vitamin A 8%; Vitamin C 26%; Calcium 4%; Iron 6%

Diet Exchanges: 4 Fruit, 1 Fat

Chunky Cinnamon Applesauce

■ 8 servings ■

SLOW COOKER:
3 1/2- to 6-quart

PREP TIME:
20 minutes

COOK TIME:
High 1 1/2 to 2 hours

Betty's Success Tip

We liked the chunkiness of this applesauce, but if you and your family like a smoother sauce, use a potato masher to break up the apple pieces.

Serving Suggestion

Warm applesauce topped with a splash of heavy whipping cream makes a memorable homemade dessert. But applesauce also is good served with your favorite pork recipe or as a topping for pancakes or waffles.

Finishing Touch

For a pretty delicate red applesauce that is packed with cinnamon flavor, stir 1/3 cup red cinnamon candies into the applesauce during the last 30 minutes of cooking.

8 medium Granny Smith apples or other tart cooking apples, peeled and cut into fourths

2/3 cup sugar

3/4 cup apple juice

2 tablespoons margarine or butter, melted

1 teaspoon ground cinnamon

1. Mix all ingredients in 3 1/2- to 6-quart slow cooker.

2. Cover and cook on high heat setting 1 1/2 to 2 hours or until apples begin to break up. Stir well to break up larger pieces of apples.

3. Serve warm or chilled. To chill, cool about 2 hours, then spoon sauce into container; cover and refrigerate until chilled.

1 Serving: Calories 170 (Calories from Fat 25); Fat 3g (Saturated 1g); Cholesterol 0mg; Sodium 40mg; Carbohydrate 39g (Dietary Fiber 3g); Protein 0g

% Daily Value: Vitamin A 4%; Vitamin C 4%; Calcium 0%; Iron 2%

Diet Exchanges: 1 1/2 Fruit, 1/2 Fat

Dried Apricot-Cherry Compote

■ *6 servings* ■

SLOW COOKER:
2- to 3 1/2-quart

PREP TIME:
5 minutes

COOK TIME:
Low 8 to 10 hours

Ingredient Substitution

For a "golden" compote, use golden raisins instead of the dried cherries.

Serving Suggestion

This compote stands on its own for dessert, but it also makes a delicious topping for orange sherbet or vanilla or chocolate ice cream.

Finishing Touch

For an added hint of orange, stir a couple of tablespoons of orange-flavored liqueur into the compote before serving.

2 packages (6 ounces each) dried apricots

2 cans (5 1/2 ounces each) apricot nectar

1/2 cup sweetened dried cherries

1/3 cup sugar

2 teaspoons grated orange peel

1. Mix all ingredients in 2- to 3 1/2-quart slow cooker.

2. Cover and cook on low heat setting 8 to 10 hours.

3. Serve warm or chilled. To chill, cool about 2 hours, then spoon compote into container; cover and refrigerate until chilled.

1 Serving: Calories 235 (Calories from Fat 0); Fat 0g (Saturated 0g); Cholesterol 0mg; Sodium 10mg; Carbohydrate 65g (Dietary Fiber 9g); Protein 3g

% Daily Value: Vitamin A 48%; Vitamin C 10%; Calcium 4%; Iron 16%

Diet Exchanges: 1 Fruit

Maple-Sauced Pears

6 servings

SLOW COOKER:
3 1/2- to 5-quart

PREP TIME:
10 minutes

COOK TIME:
High 2 to 2 1/2 hours

FINISHING COOK TIME:
High 10 minutes

6 pears

1/2 cup packed brown sugar

1/3 cup maple-flavored syrup

1 tablespoon margarine or butter, melted

1 teaspoon grated orange peel

1/8 teaspoon ground ginger

1 tablespoon cornstarch

2 tablespoons orange juice

Ingredient Substitution

For a honey of a pear, use 1/4 cup honey instead of the maple syrup for a sweet change of pace.

Finishing Touch

For an elegant dessert, place each pear upright on a pretty dessert plate. Spoon the sauce around the pear, and sprinkle with chopped toasted nuts or coconut. Spoon a big dollop of soft whipped cream alongside the pear, and garnish the plate with a twisted orange slice.

1. Peel pears. Core pears from bottom, leaving stems attached. Place pears upright in 3 1/2- to 5-quart slow cooker.

2. Mix remaining ingredients except cornstarch and orange juice; pour over pears.

3. Cover and cook on high heat setting 2 to 2 1/2 hours or until tender.

4. Remove pears from cooker; place upright in serving dish or individual dessert dishes.

5. Mix cornstarch and orange juice; stir into sauce in cooker. Cover and cook on high heat setting about 10 minutes or until sauce is thickened. Spoon sauce over pears.

1 Serving: Calories 225 (Calories from Fat 25); Fat 3g (Saturated 0g); Cholesterol 0mg; Sodium 35mg; Carbohydrate 52g (Dietary Fiber 3g); Protein 1g

% Daily Value: Vitamin A 2%; Vitamin C 6%; Calcium 4%; Iron 4%

Diet Exchanges: 3 1/2 Fruit, 1/2 Fat

Caramel Rice Pudding

■ 8 servings ■

SLOW COOKER:
2- to 3 1/2-quart

PREP TIME:
5 minutes

COOK TIME:
Low 3 to 4 hours

3 cups cooked white rice

1/2 cup raisins

1 teaspoon vanilla

1 can (14 ounces) sweetened condensed milk

1 can (12 ounces) evaporated milk

1 tablespoon sugar

1 teaspoon ground cinnamon

1. Spray inside of 2- to 3 1/2-quart slow cooker with cooking spray.

2. Mix all ingredients except sugar and cinnamon in cooker.

3. Cover and cook on low heat setting 3 to 4 hours or until liquid is absorbed. Stir pudding.

4. Sprinkle pudding with sugar and cinnamon. Serve warm.

1 Serving: Calories 385 (Calories from Fat 70); Fat 8g (Saturated 5g); Cholesterol 30mg; Sodium 140mg; Carbohydrate 68g (Dietary Fiber 1g); Protein 11g

% Daily Value: Vitamin A 8%; Vitamin C 2%; Calcium 34%; Iron 6%

Diet Exchanges: Not recommended

Betty's Success Tip

The sweetened condensed milk caramelizes during the long, slow cooking to give this rice pudding a pleasant caramel flavor and rich beige color. The evaporated milk and condensed milk also make a smooth, creamy pudding because they don't break down and separate like fresh milk would during the long cooking time.

Ingredient Substitution

This all-time favorite comfort food lends itself to a little flavor variety. Try chopped dried apricots, sweetened dried cherries or dried cranberries in place of the raisins.

Chocolate Rice Pudding

Crowd SIZE

SLOW COOKER:
3 1/2- to 6-quart

PREP TIME:
10 minutes

COOK TIME:
Low 2 1/2 to 3 hours

Betty's Success Tip

We found that using uncooked rice made a rice pudding that was sticky instead of creamy. To save time at the last minute, cook the rice ahead and keep it in the refrigerator until you are ready to make the pudding.

Finishing Touch

Dress up this creamy chocolate rice pudding with a dollop of whipped cream, sliced toasted almonds and a long-stemmed maraschino cherry

4 cups cooked white rice

3/4 cup sugar

1/4 cup baking cocoa

3 tablespoons margarine or butter, melted

1 teaspoon vanilla

2 cans (12 ounces each) evaporated milk

1. Spray inside of 3 1/2- to 6-quart slow cooker with cooking spray.

2. Mix all ingredients in cooker.

3. Cover and cook on low heat setting 2 1/2 to 3 hours or until liquid is absorbed. Stir before serving.

4. Serve warm or chilled. To chill, cool about 2 hours, then spoon pudding into container; cover and refrigerate until chilled.

1 Serving: Calories 230 (Calories from Fat 65); Fat 7g (Saturated 3g); Cholesterol 10mg; Sodium 85mg; Carbohydrate 38g (Dietary Fiber 1g); Protein 5g

% Daily Value: Vitamin A 6%; Vitamin C 0%; Calcium 10%; Iron 6%

Diet Exchanges: 1 Starch, 1 Fruit, 1/2 Skim Milk, 1 Fat

Triple Chocolate Bread Pudding

■ 8 servings ■

SLOW COOKER:
3 1/2- to 6-quart

PREP TIME:
10 minutes

COOK TIME:
High 2 1/2 to 3 hours

Ingredient Substitution

If chocolate bread isn't available, use French bread cubes. Double the chocolate chips to 1 cup so there is more chocolate flavor. It may not be triple chocolate, but it still will be triple delicious!

Finishing Touch

Turn this chocolate bread pudding into an Ultra Turtle Dessert. Top each serving with your favorite caramel sauce and a generous sprinkle of toasted pecans.

6 cups chocolate bread cubes (12 to 14 slices bread)

1/2 cup semisweet chocolate chips

1 cup fat-free cholesterol-free egg product

3/4 cup warm water

1 teaspoon vanilla

1/2 teaspoon ground cinnamon

1 can (14 ounces) chocolate sweetened condensed milk

1. Spray inside of 3 1/2- to 6-quart slow cooker with cooking spray.

2. Place bread cubes in cooker. Sprinkle with chocolate chips.

3. Mix remaining ingredients; pour over bread cubes and chocolate chips.

4. Cover and cook on high heat setting 2 1/2 to 3 hours or until toothpick inserted in center comes out clean.

5. Serve warm.

1 Serving: Calories 455 (Calories from Fat 110); Fat 12g (Saturated 7g); Cholesterol 20mg; Sodium 260mg; Carbohydrate 74g (Dietary Fiber 3g); Protein 13g

% Daily Value: Vitamin A 6%; Vitamin C 2%; Calcium 20%; Iron 6%

Diet Exchanges: Not recommended

White Chocolate Bread Pudding

Substitute French bread cubes for the chocolate bread, regular sweetened condensed milk for the chocolate milk and either 6 ounces white baking bars, coarsely chopped, or 1 cup white baking chips for the chocolate chips. Omit the cinnamon.

Cinnamon-Raisin Bread Pudding

■ 8 servings ■

SLOW COOKER:
3 1/2- to 6-quart

PREP TIME:
10 minutes

COOK TIME:
High 2 1/2 to 3 hours

6 cups cinnamon-raisin bread cubes (12 to 14 slices bread)

1/2 cup raisins

1 cup fat-free cholesterol-free egg product

3/4 cup warm water

1 teaspoon vanilla

1/2 teaspoon ground cinnamon

1 can (14 ounces) sweetened condensed milk

1. Spray inside of 3 1/2- to 6-quart slow cooker with cooking spray.

2. Place bread cubes in cooker. Sprinkle with raisins.

3. Mix remaining ingredients; pour over bread cubes and raisins.

4. Cover and cook on high heat setting 2 1/2 to 3 hours or until toothpick inserted in center comes out clean.

5. Serve warm.

1 Serving: Calories 355 (Calories from Fat 65); Fat 7g (Saturated 4g); Cholesterol 25mg; Sodium 340mg; Carbohydrate 64g (Dietary Fiber 2g); Protein 11g

% Daily Value: Vitamin A 6%; Vitamin C 2%; Calcium 24%; Iron 12%

Diet Exchanges: Not recommended

Betty's Success Tip

Using bread that is a day or two old is best; it will be firmer and drier than fresh bread. Bread that is too fresh and soft will give you a bread pudding that is too moist and soggy. We use an egg substitute because it is pasteurized, making it safe for long, slow cooking.

Ingredient Substitution

Cinnamon-raisin bread adds a little more flavor to the pudding, but cubed French bread also makes an excellent pudding. If using French bread, you may want to increase the raisins to 3/4 cup and the cinnamon to 3/4 teaspoon.

Serving Suggestion

Did you know that bread pudding is great to serve at a brunch or weekend breakfast? Top each serving with a pat of butter to melt into the hot pudding, and pass a pitcher of warm maple syrup to drizzle on top. What a way to start the day!

Helpful Nutrition
and Cooking Information

Nutrition Guidelines:

We provide nutrition information for each recipe that includes calories, fat, cholesterol, sodium, carbohydrate, fiber and protein. Individual food choices can be based on this information

Recommended intake for a daily diet of 2,000 calories as set by the Food and Drug Administration

Total Fat	Less than 65g
Saturated Fat	Less than 20g
Cholesterol	Less than 300mg
Sodium	Less than 2,400mg
Total Carbohydrate	300g
Dietary Fiber	25g

Criteria Used for Calculating Nutrition Information:

The first ingredient was used wherever a choice is given (such as 1/3 cup sour cream or plain yogurt).

The first ingredient amount was used wherever a range is given (such as 3 to 3 1/2 pound cut-up broiler-fryer chicken).

The first serving number was used wherever a range is given (such as 4 to 6 servings).

"If desired" ingredients (such as sprinkle with brown sugar if desired) and recipe variations were *not* included .

Only the amount of a marinade or frying oil that is estimated to be absorbed by the food during preparation or cooking was calculated.

Ingredients Used in Recipe Testing and Nutrition Calculations:

- Ingredients used for testing represent those that the majority of consumers use in their homes: large eggs, 2% milk, 80% lean ground beef, canned ready-to-use chicken broth, and vegetable oil spread containing *not less than 65% fat*.

- Fat-free, low-fat or low-sodium products are not used, unless otherwise indicated.

- Solid vegetable shortening (not butter, margarine, nonstick cooking sprays or vegetable oil spread as they can cause sticking problems) is used to grease pans, unless otherwise indicated.

Equipment Used in Recipe Testing:

We use equipment for testing that the majority of consumers use in their homes. If a specific piece of equipment (such as a wire whisk) is necessary for recipe success, it will be listed in the recipe.

- Cookware and bakeware **without** nonstick coatings were used, unless otherwise indicated.

- No dark colored, black or insulated bakeware was used.

- When a baking *pan* is specified in a recipe, a *metal* pan was used; a baking *dish* or pie *plate* means ovenproof glass was used.

- An electric hand mixer was used for mixing *only when mixer speeds are specified* in the recipe directions. When a mixer speed is not given, a spoon or fork was used.

Cooking Terms Glossary:

Beat: Mix ingredients vigorously with spoon, fork, wire whisk, hand beater or electric mixer until smooth and uniform.

Boil: Heat liquid until bubbles rise continuously and break on the surface and steam is given off. For rolling boil, the bubbles form rapidly.

Chop: Cut into coarse or fine irregular pieces with a knife, food chopper, blender or food processor.

Cube: Cut into squares 1/2 inch or larger.

Dice: Cut into squares smaller than 1/2 inch.

Grate: Cut into tiny particles using small rough holes of grater (citrus peel or chocolate).

Grease: Rub the inside surface of a pan with shortening, using pastry brush, piece of waxed paper or paper towel, to prevent food from sticking during baking (as for some casseroles).

Julienne: Cut into thin, matchlike strips, using knife or food processor (vegetables, fruits, meats).

Mix: Combine ingredients in any way that distributes them evenly.

Sauté: Cook foods in hot oil or margarine over medium-high heat with frequent tossing and turning motion.

Shred: Cut into long thin pieces by rubbing food across the holes of a shredder, as for cheese, or by using a knife to slice very thinly, as for cabbage.

Simmer: Cook in liquid just below the boiling point on top of the stove; usually after reducing heat from a boil. Bubbles will rise slowly and break just below the surface.

Stir: Mix ingredients until uniform consistency. Stir once in a while for stirring occasionally, often for stirring frequently and continuously for stirring constantly.

Toss: Tumble ingredients lightly with a lifting motion (such as green salad), usually to coat evenly or mix with another food.

Metric Conversion Guide

Volume

U.S. Units	Canadian Metric	Australian Metric
1/4 teaspoon	1 mL	1 ml
1/2 teaspoon	2 mL	2 ml
1 teaspoon	5 mL	5 ml
1 tablespoon	15 mL	20 ml
1/4 cup	50 mL	60 ml
1/3 cup	75 mL	80 ml
1/2 cup	125 mL	125 ml
2/3 cup	150 mL	170 ml
3/4 cup	175 mL	190 ml
1 cup	250 mL	250 ml
1 quart	1 liter	1 liter
1 1/2 quarts	1.5 liters	1.5 liters
2 quarts	2 liters	2 liters
2 1/2 quarts	2.5 liters	2.5 liters
3 quarts	3 liters	3 liters
4 quarts	4 liters	4 liters

Weight

U.S. Units	Canadian Metric	Australian Metric
1 ounce	30 grams	30 grams
2 ounces	55 grams	60 grams
3 ounces	85 grams	90 grams
4 ounces (1/4 pound)	115 grams	125 grams
8 ounces (1/2 pound)	225 grams	225 grams
16 ounces (1 pound)	455 grams	500 grams
1 pound	455 grams	1/2 kilogram

Measurements

Inches	Centimeters
1	2.5
2	5.0
3	7.5
4	10.0
5	12.5
6	15.0
7	17.5
8	20.5
9	23.0
10	25.5
11	28.0
12	30.5
13	33.0

Temperatures

Fahrenheit	Celsius
32°	0°
212°	100°
250°	120°
275°	140°
300°	150°
325°	160°
350°	180°
375°	190°
400°	200°
425°	220°
450°	230°
475°	240°
500°	260°

Note: The recipes in this cookbook have not been developed or tested using metric measures. When converting recipes to metric, some variations in quality may be noted.

Index

Numbers in **bold italics** indicate photos.

C

Cabbage
 apple, and pork salad, warm, 83
 and pork soup, savory, 22, **23**
 red, with apples, 162
 Roll Casserole, 76
 tips on shredding, 17, 162
Cake, hot fudge sundae, 200, **201**
Canadian bacon soup, savory lentil and, 26, **27**
Cannellini bean, veal and, soup, Italian, 28
Caramelized Onion Pot Roast, 60, **61**
 leftover recipes from, 62, 63
Caramel Rice Pudding, 210, **211**
Carrot(s)
 bulgur pilaf with broccoli and, 156, **157**
 and Celery Relish, 174, **175**
Casserole
 barley-pine nut, 152, **153**
 cabbage roll, 76
 herbed turkey and wild rice, 120, **121**
 layered turkey and sweet potato, 127
 lentil and mixed-vegetable, **136,** 154
Cassoulet, turkey sausage, 133
Celery, carrot and, relish, 174, **175**
Cheese, feta, turkey breast with bulgur and, 128
Cheese-Beer Dip, 186
Cheesy Bean Dip, 187
Cheesy Broiled French Bread, 16
Cherry
 apricot-, dried, compote, 207
 Cobbler, 202, **203**
 peach-, chutney, 178, **179**
Chicken
 breasts, Italian sun-dried, 109
 in Brunswick Stew, 38
 with green chili rice, Mexican, 110, **111**
 Legs with Herbed Onion Sauce, 117
 mango chutney, curry, 112, **113**
 Moroccan, 118, **119**
 in Red Wine, 115
 and Rice Gumbo Soup, 18, **19**
 Stew with Pepper and Pineapple, 36, **37**
 Stroganoff Pot Pie, 106, **107**
 and stuffing supper, herbed 114
 Thai, **104,** 116
 and wild rice, creamy, 108
Chili
 chunky pork and beef sausage, 53
 family favorite, 52
 green, chicken with, rice, Mexican, 110, **111**
 spicy pork, 87
 turkey and brown rice, 49
 vegetarian, with baked tortilla strips, 50, **51**
Chocolate
 bread pudding, triple, 213
 Fondue, 198, **199**
 Rice Pudding, 212
Chowder
 peppery fish, with rice, 35
 potato and double corn, 34
Chunky Cinnamon Applesauce, 206
Chunky Pork and Beef Sausage Chili, 53
Chutney
 golden fruit, 177
 mango, chicken curry, 112, **113**
 peach-cherry, 178, **179**
Cider
 apple. See Wassail
 spiced cran-apple, 193
Cilantro, about, 132
Cinnamon applesauce, chunky, 206
Cinnamon-Raisin Bread Pudding, 214, **215**
Cobbler, cherry, 202, **203**
Cocoa
 in Hot Fudge Sundae Cake, 200, **201**
 mocha, 194, **195**
Compote, dried apricot-cherry, 207
Conserve, pear-orange, 180, **181**
Continuous slow cooker, 7
Cooking terms, 217
Corn
 double, potato and, chowder, 34
 scalloped, 163
Cornmeal dumplings, turkey and vegetables with, 129
Corn Relish, 176
Crab, artichoke-, spread, 192
Cran-apple cider, spiced, 193
Cranberry(ies)
 Baked Apples, 205
 gravy, brisket with, 64
 wild rice and, turkey breast stuffed with, 124, **125**
 wild rice with, 138
Creamy Chicken and Wild Rice, 108
Creamy Leek and Potato Soup, 15
Creamy Wild Rice, 172
Cuban Black Beans and Rice, 142, **143**
Curried Fruit, 182
Curry, mango chutney chicken, 112, **113**

D

Dijon, lamb, 95
Dip
 butterscotch-rum, 197
 cheese-beer, 186
 cheesy bean, 187
Dressing, plum, 83